FINDING FREEDOM IN GOD'S ILLOGICAL WAYS

A JOURNEY OF DISCOVERIES

by
Sister Mary Francis Power, ESEH

Illustrated by
Mary McDonald

1

Published by Eudist Press International

THE
EUDISTS
CONGREGATION OF
JESUS AND MARY

PO Box 3619
Vista, CA 92085
www.eudistsusa.org

Finding freedom in the realization that life is not about me.

Think differently.

Embrace change.

Man's logic and reason are not the same as God's.

Think differently.

Let him be in charge.

Listen with the ears of my heart.

Think differently.

Finding freedom from old baggage and old pain.

Discover what he has waiting for me.

Think differently, discover unconditional love, find freedom.

DEDICATION

To my beloved sons, Chris, Joey and Bobby. My heart and love will always be with you, your wonderful wives, Vanessa, Karen, and Robyn, and your adorable children, Olivia, Benicio, Luna, Dean, and Dimara. I appreciate your patience with my drastic and seemingly curious changes in this later stage of life.

To my siblings, Sue, Donna, Dot, Mike, Jimmy, Jackie, Bobby, Mary, and their families, all who have been patiently awaiting an understanding of the changes I chose to make. To my brothers-in-law and sisters-in-law, for loving my siblings. And to all my nieces and nephews, for taking care of their parents and siblings.

There are over seventy divine creations in our McDonald clan, too many to list here! I love you all dearly.

Prayers are rendered daily for all of you, as well as my sons' father, Dean; my father and mother, Bill and Evy; my sister, Becky; and all our family members who have gone to their eternal rest. May you rest peacefully in the arms of Our Lord.

To devout practicing Christian friends who played pivotal roles on my faith journey, including Babi, Marsha, Diana, Jen, Shaun, Scott, Father Brian, Reese, Trish, Hortencia, and Sister Dolores. You are bright lights of Christ who will never fully know what your good counsel has done for me. I have a new life, renewed in Jesus Christ, because of your unconditional love. You either directly advised me, or demonstrated true Christian values and virtues, and for this I am especially grateful.

There are no words sufficient enough to thank my spiritual director and good friend, Father Richard Wise, whose sage guidance keeps me continually focused. Father is a good and faithful servant, "a priest's priest," meaning that he has mentored many younger priests on their journeys. He inspires everyone around him to become more holy, imitating the way, the truth, and the life of Jesus. His always-present sense of humor lightens our hearts, and gives us a fresh perspective of our circumstances. May many priests follow his delightful priestly example.

Finally, this book is also dedicated to the Eudist Servants of the Eleventh Hour (ESEH) Foundress, Mother Antonia Brenner, ESEH; Delegate of the Tijuana Archbishop to the ESEH, Father John Howard, CJM; General Leader, Sister Viola Ramirez, ESEH; former General Leader, Sister Judith Krantz, ESEH; my fellow sisters; and future candidates. I am grateful to have been led by God to this association of the faithful of consecrated sisters, and especially thankful for the formation efforts of Sister Lillian Manning, ESEH, and Sister John Mary Schweikardt, ESEH.

In Memory Of

Mother Antonia Brenner
Eudist Servants of the Eleventh Hour
December 1, 1926 – October 17, 2013

Father John Howard
Congregation of Jesus and Mary
December 27, 1940 – February 23, 2021

TABLE OF CONTENTS

PREFACE

C ontained within this spiritual autobiography are divine promptings to my soul, promptings that came throughout my faith journey. These promptings were meant for me, and are not messages for the whole world. I share them only as part of my faith journey with God.

On the day of my calling to become a sister, Jesus[1] also told me to "write the book." That was in 2010. He did not tell me *what* to write until 2019. He did not give me the *reason* he wanted me to write the book until the morning of writing chapter thirteen, in 2020.

He started pushing me to write in 2018. Still, I did not begin. I was not motivated, because I did not know what to write, I never wrote a book before, and I did not have the time to write. The task seemed overwhelming.

Following is the account of the event of the *Last Drop*, which is what it took for me to finally become motivated.

---

[1] References are made to the members of the Most Holy Trinity throughout this book – the Father, Son, and the Holy Spirit of God, and it is the central mystery of the Christian faith and life (*Catechism of the Catholic Church*, 2nd ed., 232-237, 261). On this journey I welcomed Jesus Christ to become my best friend, then began to hear his voice (internally) two months later. The *Catechism of the Catholic Church* will hereafter be referred to as CCC.

Last Drop

In the summer of 2019, before the COVID-19 pandemic, it began. I received confirmation from Jesus again that it was time to write the book.

Tuesday. When I approached the Extraordinary Minister of Communion during Mass to receive the Precious Blood of Jesus, she said, "Sister, this is the last drop." Her words moved me, especially when I knelt at my pew afterward to pray, to talk with Jesus himself, as I normally do. Many thoughts came to me. The most prominent was, "What if this was the last drop of his Precious Blood?" That would mean that if there are no priests after this last drop, there can be no consecration of the bread and wine to become the Precious Body and Precious Blood of Jesus.[2]

What if today is the day of the last drop of the Precious Blood of Jesus available *anywhere in the world*, and there are no priests to consecrate wine into the Precious Blood during Mass? Why is this a terrifying thought?[3]

Wednesday. On the morning of this day, I thought, "Surely, I will not receive the last drop of His Precious Blood today?" I anticipated nothing as I drove to church that morning. When I received the cup from the Extraordinary Minister,

---

[2] "By the consecration, the transubstantiation of the bread and wine into the Body and Blood of Christ is brought about. Under the consecrated species of bread and wine, Christ himself, living and glorious, is present in a true, real and substantial manner: His Body and Blood, with his soul and divinity." (CCC 1413; see also, Council of Trent: DS 1640, 1651).

[3] The Eucharist spiritually feeds the faithful and unites us with the Church in heaven, the Blessed Virgin Mary, and all the saints. "Having passed from this world to the Father, Christ gives us in the Eucharist the pledge of glory with him. Participation in the Holy Sacrifice identifies us with his Heart, sustains our strength along the pilgrimage of this life, makes us long for eternal life, and unites us even now to the Church in heaven, the Blessed Virgin Mary, and all the saints." (CCC 1419).

I noticed it was the last drop *again*. It was not enough to leave for the next person in line. I consumed it entirely and returned the cup to the Extraordinary Minister. I walked to my pew, knelt, and contemplated how this could be. Again, I consumed the last drop of His Precious Blood.

I was receiving awakening thoughts, thinking of the possibility of losing priests, and considering the decreasing number of priests in Mexico.[4] Those who speak from the pulpit against violence, drug wars, human trafficking, and prostitution, can become murder victims.

Additionally, in the summer of 2018, Catholics endured the pain of learning [once again] about former priest scandals and coverups that had taken place mostly many years ago.[5] Some frustrated and disappointed priests—the very ones needed to celebrate the Eucharist at every Mass—left the Church. Some seminarians who aspired to become priests also left.

Today, anyone who desires to work with vulnerable individuals in the Catholic Church, must undergo a background check and obey protection guidelines. There is much more oversight for the safety of vulnerable people than there used to be. Everyone in the Church is more aware now.

On a regular basis, monthly in some dioceses, priests, deacons, brothers, sisters, and lay people who work with vulnerable people are required to study, and successfully test on material related to the protection of children.[6]

---

[4] *"1 cardinal and 57 priests killed in the last 30 years in Mexico." www.catholicnewsagency.com/news/251749/report-cardinal-and-57-priests-killed-in-the-last-30-years-in-mexico.* Mexico City newsroom, July 8, 2022. Last viewed November 4, 2022.

[5] Laurie Goodstein and Sharon Otterman, "Catholic priests abused 1,000 children in Pennsylvania, Report Says," *New York Times*, August 14, 2018, *www.nytimes.com/2018/08/14/us/catholic-church-sex-abuse-pennsylvania.html.*

[6] To learn more, visit: *Virtus® Online*, A Program and Service of The National Catholic Risk Retention Group, Inc., *www.virtusonline.org.*

There will always be a need for ordained men, and consecrated men and women. God calls them throughout the ages. What would the world be like, though, if no one said yes to the calling to become an ordained priest, and to serve those who suffer?

And what if we no longer had the opportunity to receive Jesus Christ in the Eucharist? Our Catholic faith is that Jesus Christ is *truly present* as the Precious Body and Precious Blood in the Eucharist.

Thursday. Again, as I drove to church, I had no expectations of receiving the last drop for the third day in a row. I remember thinking, "Surely, I won't receive the last drop of Precious Blood again." Well, I did.

It is impossible to predict if a person will receive the last drop when they are in line to receive him. If someone wanted to receive the last drop every day, they could not possibly calculate how to even cause this to happen. The number of people in line changes every day.

The amount of wine that is consumed by parishioners cannot be pre-measured. Parishioners sit in different places in the pews each day. Sacristans do not always pour the exact amount of wine into the containers every day.[7]

Then I heard the Holy Spirit say, "What if this was the last drop of my Precious Blood anywhere in the world?"

Friday. I knew I would not receive just one drop on Friday. It was the fourth day. For the first time in four days, I did not receive the last drop. Why? I was not meant to have it. Instead, the cup was half full. Of course, it was. Many times, God reveals things to us using the number three. Three is representative of the Most Holy Trinity[8] of the Father, Son,

---

[7] Sacristans are responsible for preparing the water and wine, along with other duties and responsibilities for the celebration of Mass. *www.ewtn.com/catholicism/library/sacristans-duties-4382.*

[8] CCC 232-237

and Holy Spirit, and the central mystery of the Christian faith and life. And we pray the Divine Mercy Chaplet at 3:00 p.m., the hour Christ died on the cross.

The most significant thought came on the fourth day. Jesus said to me, "If there are no priests left anywhere in the world, then I will have to come back."

No one knows, except God, when Jesus will return: "But of that day or that hour no one knows, not even the angels in heaven, nor the Son, but only the Father. Take heed, watch and pray; for you do not know when the time will come" (Mk. 13:32-33).[9] Our faith says he will return.

What does this potentially last drop have to do with writing a book?

On the fourth day, Jesus told me the first steps in writing the book. He said to prepare a dedicated writing space and identify a time to write. I had a weekly ministry schedule, so I would need to find time for writing, somehow.

He gave me three consecutive days of the last drop of His Precious Blood in the cup to awaken me to the unfortunate possibility of a complete absence of priests throughout the entire world. Should this happen, there would be no consecration of the bread and wine into His Precious Body and Precious Blood. This communion with him spiritually feeds devout Catholics.

Imagine learning you received the very last drop during the Mass you attended today. His Precious Blood is not found anywhere on the planet, and you had the last drop. What would that mean to you? How would your life change?

---

[9] Unless otherwise noted, all scripture verses are taken from: *The Holy Bible, Revised Standard Version, Second Catholic Edition* (Nashville, Tennessee: Thomas Nelson, 1966).

It is interesting that while I was writing this book, Catholics learned that we could not attend Mass at the church, due to the COVID-19 virus pandemic. This was happening all over the world. *We were not able to receive the Precious Body and Precious Blood of Jesus Christ.*

We were experiencing life without the *actual presence* of Jesus in our lives. We prayed the following prayer during live-streamed Mass.

Spiritual Communion Prayer

My Jesus,
I believe that you are present in the most
Holy Sacrament.
I love you above all things, and I desire to receive
you into my soul.
Since I cannot at this moment receive
you sacramentally,
Come at least spiritually into my heart.
I embrace you as though you were already there
and unite myself wholly to you.
Never permit me to be separated from you.

Amen

It was an emotional time for those of us who could not attend Mass in person.

It took three days of drinking the last drop to realize Jesus was motivating me to write this book with the intent of increasing religious vocations. He created within me an awareness of something I never considered seriously, that the day might come when there are no priests anywhere in the world to celebrate Mass. Jesus is always with us, of course; however, our faith as Catholics is enriched, knowing we receive him substantially in the celebration of the Eucharist during every Mass.

Jesus narrowed the focus even more, telling me to specifically write a memoir [spiritual autobiography] of what can happen when one middle-aged woman says yes to the calling from Jesus, to serve those who suffer.

He gave me the table of contents for the book. I sorted the documentation I kept over the years for the future writing of the book. Struggling for six months to find the time to write, God finally gave me the gift of time.

The COVID-19 sheltering-in-place began. My age of sixty-five at the time, plus underlying medical conditions, and orders from the Georgia Department of Corrections to cease all visitations to incarcerated facilities, kept me at home.

Suddenly, I had time to write the first draft all-at-once, and without distractions!

Writing this book seemed as though I was cobbling together pieces of a puzzle for Jesus himself, using me to share this journey with those who are struggling in the ways I used to – physically, spiritually, mentally, and emotionally.

The Holy Spirit tugged at my heart for ten years after the calling in 2010, as I gathered things that were spiritually inspiring, to eventually add to this book at some unforeseen time in the future. Everything was added to a box labeled "book" and remained unopened until the pandemic began.

Praying before working resulted in more well-written chapters than if I had not prayed beforehand. This is true for any effort I complete.

Once a person finishes reading this book, they will have a better idea of not only the calling, but also a faith journey itself. This journey is just one example, however. Every journey is unique.

All callings, if followed, contain ardent prayer, discernment, perseverance, patience, humility, charity, obedience, and unconditional love. If you believe you are being called to serve as an ordained priest or deacon, a consecrated brother or sister, or someone who is merely seeking ways to become more holy, I pray this book is useful to you in some way.

This account may also provide readers with the work involved in experiencing conversions of the heart, mind, and soul, freeing themselves of the things that keep them from growing spiritually, while adopting the values and virtues of Jesus Christ.

Finally, I hope this book will help families understand the journey of their loved ones who have been called to serve as ordained ministers, or consecrated religious brothers and sisters, while reading one person's spiritual autobiography.

INTRODUCTION

What happens when a middle-aged woman says "yes" to the calling from Jesus to become a nun?

Later, I would become a consecrated sister, not a nun, and technically there is a difference.[10] A simple explanation is that a nun is a woman who lives a cloistered life in a convent. A consecrated sister is a woman who works in the world, serving those who suffer. She may, or may not, live in a community.

My "yes" as a consecrated Catholic sister is like that of our Blessed Mother Mary. She said "yes" when the Angel Gabriel told her she was to have a son, and he would be the son of God. Mary's response was, "Behold, I am the handmaid of the Lord. May it be done to me according to your word" (Lk. 1:38).

Jesus gave me the original title for this book, *You Are Who You Aren't*, in 1998, over twenty years ago. During the writing process, it became the title of the first chapter. A new title that would more profoundly capture the essence of this book was created in a white board session with the professional editor, publisher, and myself: *Finding Freedom in God's Illogical Ways: A Journey of Discoveries.*

---

[10] To learn more, go to *www.vatican.va/archive/cod-iuris-canonici/cic_index_en.html*. Additionally, a simple summary of the differences between nuns and sisters is: *www.canonlawmadeeasy.com/2009/03/19/whats-the-difference-between-sisters-and-nuns.*

Just when we think we know who we are, we are already changing in some way. My journey to become a sister was composed of many inward and outward changes. I began experiencing significant spiritual events in 2008.

Another ten years went by. In January 2018, Jesus was quite direct with me, that it was time, once again, to write the book. Originally, he told me on the day of my calling in 2010 to do this. I delayed working on it because I had no motivation to do so. The thought of how much work it would be was overwhelming. I had never written a book, and frankly could not yet see how to approach the effort. Even after he urged me to begin, I still resisted. I did not know how to piece everything together into something sensible that others could understand. And I certainly did not know how to fit this work into my prison ministry schedule.

One year later, in the summer of 2019, he finally got my attention to write the book. He was about to connect the dots, so-to-speak. This time I knew I could not avoid his will for me any longer. First, he gave me an unexplained phenomenon I refer to as the "Last Drop," when I received exactly one drop of Precious Blood during Mass, three days in a row. The cup was half full on the fourth day.

The details of this story are found in the preface of this book. It was the impetus for me to get to work!

Shortly thereafter, Jesus told me to prepare a place to work, to fit this in with my ministry schedule, and also gave me the table of contents. Then he told me to sort all the materials I collected over the years into piles, according to each chapter title. It took me two months to complete the sorting because of the volume of documentation I collected. The sources of information were journals, voice recordings, Word documents, prayer cards, retreat notes, the Bible, the Catechism of the Catholic Church, and other resource books.

He then gave me the focus of this book, to help increase vocations through sharing the journey of one middle-aged woman who said "yes" to the calling.

The journey of anyone who has been called to become a priest, deacon, sister, or brother is challenging. The path came with daily goals designed to stretch us to become something we have not yet been, a better version of ourselves. The path also contained unexpected discoveries.

I believe he gave me the focus of increasing vocations because of the loss of some priests, deacons, religious, and lay persons who may have lost faith in the leadership of the Church, and subsequently chose to leave the Church.

These writings also focused on the work necessary to transition into a consecrated world, while encountering joy, peace, and fulfillment of God's will along the way. Additionally, this book may help those who wish to experience a conversion of their heart, mind, and soul. And finally, this book could be helpful to someone who has not received a religious calling, but is searching for answers at a deeper level of their faith journey.

Many men and women experience callings from Our Lord to become vessels of mercy for others, but do not know how to pursue the calling and determine what work needs to be done to answer God's call for them. In this book, I shared unexplained mystical phenomena, significant events, and wisdom gained on the journey, to help others discern their journeys.

This journey sometimes has details that are difficult to comprehend using normal reason and logic. Sometimes God's ways seem illogical. For those seeking explanations and a better understanding of what can happen, I hope this book will provide answers and somewhat satisfy curiosity.

One can keep seeking answers, never to be satisfied, or one can at some point, simply accept faith. Once this happens, everything will begin to fall in place and make sense. It did for me, and it has for billions of other practicing Christians in the world.

"Jesus then said to those Jews who believed in him, 'If you remain in my word, you will truly be my disciples, and you will know the truth, and the truth will set you free'" (Jn 8:31-32).

By writing this book, I also hope to give my family a better understanding of the journey. The calling made absolutely no sense to me at the beginning. How could I expect my family to understand this? There were far too many details and experiences that took place, to *fully* share with them along the way.

Now the journey makes sense to me, and I hope I have successfully conveyed as much as possible in this book, or at least the essence of it.

I gave accounts of personal experiences, including unexplained mystical events, from before and after becoming a sister. These experiences were unlike anything I encountered in my former life.

Receiving a genuine calling to become a sister was never my plan. I did not anticipate this in any way. I did not see this coming. As I have told many people, "God had to hit me upside the head with a 2x4 [piece of lumber]" in a manner of speaking, to get my attention.

My journey was like the story of Saul of Tarsus in the Bible, who underwent a conversion of heart, mind, and soul, to become Saint Paul, the Apostle. Jesus had to knock me off my high horse too.

There was no rational explanation for what was happening.

At the time I received the calling from Jesus, I was a manager in a federal agency, with many responsibilities as an official of the federal government. I worked up to the level of a GS-14, civil servant, and at one point was considered for promotion to a GS-15; respectively, equivalency of Colonel and General, depending upon the description of duties, pay scales, the organization itself, and other factors.

I achieved many things as a government employee, but the work was not joyful.

My career required me to constantly use reason and logic to perform my duties, to produce results. At one point, my annual salary was over six figures with full benefits and generous leave accruals. I worked long hours, even working overtime without pay because there were not enough funds in the budget to pay for this.

I was not an alcoholic or abused drugs. *This gives you some idea of my mental capacity at the time of my calling.* It was a sudden, unexplained phenomena. I learned later that this is one way God works. "For my thoughts are not your thoughts; neither are your ways, my ways" (Is. 55:8).

To us, his ways seem illogical and unreasonable.

God does not measure the way we measure. His idea of fairness is not the same as ours. Our expectation of reason is not God's way of reasoning. We use math and science to work through problems. Those who have set out to prove the non-existence of God have never been able to do so, because his ways are not our ways. He is of the supernatural realm. Even the definition of faith can be challenging to understand, "Faith is the realization of what is hoped for and evidence of things not seen" (Heb. 11:1).

Faith often seems illogical, requiring us to suspend our reliance on logic.[11]

To say "yes" to this calling, the only thing I needed was faith as small as a mustard seed, though I did not know it then. As with many things, it would all become clear with time. The gift of faith from God, as small as it was, helped me to grow spiritually. "If you have faith as small as a mustard seed, you can say to this mountain, move from here to there, and it will move" (Mt. 17:20).

Of course, this does not mean that I will move a mountain. It means that "with God, all things are possible" (Mt. 19:26). I can now say that I have done things on this journey I never thought possible had it not been for God helping me.

As far back as I can remember, I always believed in God. He first tapped me on the shoulder when I was fourteen years old, placing the desire on my heart to become a nun.

Why had I not become a nun in my earlier years? Like most other young girls, I discovered boys. At seventeen years of age, I was engaged, and at nineteen, I married. My husband and I joined the United States Air Force together when I was twenty years old. Later, I separated from the military to start our family. We raised three sons, earned our Bachelor's degrees, and grew our careers. Unfortunately, later we would divorce, go our separate ways, and neither of us remarried.

While I was married, I was in a vocation of marriage, under the Sacrament of Matrimony according to the Catholic Church. One cannot be married and be a sister at the same time.[12] I was raising my sons with my husband while

---

[11] Steve Marshall, Mission Advancement Director, and Theologian, The Eudists – Congregation of Jesus and Mary.

[12] Believe it or not, a few women have asked me if they could be a sister while they were married. In our association a woman must be single, divorced with an annulment, or a widow.

I learned new skills of administration, personnel, accounting, policy, and management.

After the divorce and as an empty nester, there was plenty of time to be in the stillness after working hours, totally alone. God gave me this time in the silence as a special gift. I refer to it as my sabbatical. It was the phase of my life to sit and ponder existence, purpose in life, take time to discern many things, *begin making new discoveries*, and wonder at the beauty of the world God created for us.

I received the calling on August 6, 2010, when I was visiting my mother. I was fifty-five years old. At that time, I was a divorced mother of three grown sons, no dependents living with me, and a manager in a federal agency. *Realizing that call concretely was one discovery.*

God doesn't care what age you are when he calls you to do his work.

Searching for a traditional order, no one would accept me because of my age and history of medical conditions. Finally, God led me to the Eudist Servants of the Eleventh Hour,[13] an association of the faithful of consecrated sisters who are called late in life. Most of our sisters are mothers and grandmothers who are retired and financially self-sufficient. *Led by God to find these sisters was another discovery.*

After much prayer and discernment, I retired in November 2011 to follow this calling. Today, God uses my life experiences to help the least of our brothers and sisters in their struggles. *Each new encounter is a discovery of someone deeply loved by God, and a new opportunity to express that love to them.*

The title of this book: *Finding Freedom in God's Illogical Ways: A Journey of Discoveries*, can apply to every human life,

---

[13] For more information about the Eudist Servants, visit *www.eudistservants.org*. Also, chapter 5 of this book, *Searching For An Order*, goes into the specific details of how God led me to them.

even if a person does not have a religious calling, because we all have the opportunity to change for the better.

From conception to natural death, we continually change in many ways. Additionally, we have the most important opportunity to change our hearts, minds, and souls, as long as we are open to change. *We can continually become a better version of ourselves, discover new freedom, even — especially — in God's illogical ways.*

My life changed in drastic ways I thought were not possible after I welcomed Jesus into my heart to develop a personal relationship with him. Although the changes I made seemed illogical and unreasonable, I chose to make these changes anyway. That choice was possible through an attitude similar to the one expressed in the following text reported to be a favorite of Saint Teresa of Calcutta (formerly known as Mother Teresa):

<u>Do It Anyway</u>[14]

People are often unreasonable, illogical and self-centered;
Forgive them anyway.
If you are kind, people may accuse you of selfish, ulterior motives;
Be kind anyway.
If you are successful, you will win some false friends and some true enemies;

---

[14] This text is often attributed to Mother Teresa and harmonizes beautifully with her spirituality. It was on a poster hung in her children's home of Shishu Bhavan in Calcutta, according to A Simple Path by Lucinda Vardey (New York: Ballantine, 1995). This book was the first published connection of the text with the saint. In the form cited by Vardey, it was a modified version of Kent M. Keith's "Paradoxical Commandments," which he first published in his pamphlet The Silent Revolution: Dynamic Leadership in the Student Council, 4th edition (Cambridge, MA: Harvard Student Agencies, 1968).

Succeed anyway.
If you are honest and frank, people may cheat you;
Be honest and frank anyway.
What you spend years building, someone could destroy overnight;
Build anyway.
If you find serenity and happiness, they may be jealous;
Be happy anyway.
The good you do today, people will often forget tomorrow;
Do good anyway.
Give the world the best you have, and it may never be enough;
Give the world the best you've got anyway.
You see, in the final analysis, it is between you and your God;
It was never between you and them anyway.

I will frequently refer to God, Jesus, Mary, and the Holy Spirit, in this book, as they have been very close to me on this journey. In our faith as Catholics, we believe Jesus Christ is the long-awaited Messiah, incarnate of God himself, and the Holy Spirit of God. The Father, Son, and Holy Spirit are the Most Holy Trinity of God, and this is the central mystery of the Christian faith and life.[15]

I give my witness in this book.

I did not plan, expect, or ask God for any of the incredible events of my journey. They are courtesy of God himself. I am grateful to him for showing me how to become a better version of myself. Most especially, I am thankful for the unexpected joy he had waiting for me that results in serving others, while not expecting anything in return.

---

[15] CCC 232-237

Finally, and most importantly, in the earlier drafts of this book, the Holy Spirit whispered to me that this book would become a legacy to my children and their families.

May the Lord bless you, protect you from all evil, and bring you to everlasting life.

Sister Mary Francis Power, ESEH

CHAPTER 1
YOU ARE WHO YOU AREN'T

Henry David Thoreau said, "Things do not change. We change." It is the same with God. He never changes. We change.

As soon as we think we know who we are, we have already begun to change. From the moment of conception in our mother's womb to the natural death of the physical body, we can expect nothing but change. Life itself is a series of changes. From the beginning of a human being's life, the cells of a newly-forming baby change many times before the birth of the fully formed person.

Physically, we may also inherit genetic history from our parents that can cause changes in our lives, such as inheriting a disease that can impact one's life. Mentally and emotionally, we can become products of the influences of our environments. What we read, who we listen to, and what we watch on television and social media are all sources of information we receive and process. At times we can make changes ourselves, or sometimes changes are imposed on us by others.

We can embrace change or fight change. We can work with others to bring about functional changes. We can also choose to protest all changes that might affect our lives if we are someone who does not like *any* kind of change. *Discerning the reason for the change is essential for each person to consider.*

Most of the time, I welcome change, seeing it as an adventure, a breath of fresh air in my life. Other times change is difficult to accept.

When I was growing up, I had low self-esteem, was extremely shy, insecure, and had no self-confidence. I learned later though, that God will always have more confidence in us than we will ever have in ourselves.

At that time, I did not realize that I could excel at anything. I was number three of eleven children. Most of my childhood was spent cooking, cleaning, and caring for younger children. And there was little time for anything else. It was not until I started college that I realized I could excel if I applied myself.

My fiancé would later tell me, "You can make A's and B's just like anybody else. You just have to get inside the teacher's head to find out what they want you to learn." He and I graduated together from Warner Robins High School, Warner Robins, Georgia. He was an honor roll student. I was not. Later, in college, I did in fact, finally achieve A's and B's, thanks to his encouragement, and my determination to improve myself. These were good changes in my life.

My siblings and I are very proud of the accomplishments of our father and mother. Our mother was the most selfless person we ever knew. She and my father grew up on Iowa farms during the Great Depression, having very little. They had their Catholic faith and a strong work ethic. They were family-oriented. They, too, experienced many changes in their lives.

When my siblings and I were growing up, Dad received reassignment orders to relocate every 2-4 years, moving from one Air Force base to another. Our father was a United States Air Force Pilot for thirty-three years (part of this time as Army Air Corps). He was an instructor pilot to men who flew in World War II. He was in the Korean War and actively served in the Vietnam War. He served his country well. He was one of the founding fathers of Air Rescue missions as a Wing Commander of the Air Rescue and Recovery Squadron at Wheelus Air Force Base, Tripoli, Libya.

Most of my siblings and I were born on Air Force bases. Every time Dad was reassigned to a new base, we moved into a different school system. It was challenging to maintain consistent learning from one school to another. We learned to adapt quickly, which is a good skill to have! It seemed as though we were constantly in a preparedness mode, always awaiting new changes.

Dad would tell us, "poor planning," if our outcomes failed due to poor planning. It is still a running joke in our family, although we always took Dad's guidance seriously.

How does change affect our lives? We continuously change in ways we are not even aware of. Some changes are life-giving; other changes can end our lives. Some changes are unsettling, some are difficult to do. Change can also be liberating, exciting, and fun.

Do we embrace change, or reject change? How do we process changes we know are coming? Will this change make my life better or worse? Will this change make me a better or worse person? How will this change affect my relationships?

We never know what changes are in store for us. Expect that every new day will bring change. As a practicing Catholic, I embrace change if I can, *but only if* it is consistent with Catholic values and virtues. I endeavor to reject change if it is inconsistent with the way, the truth, and the life of Jesus.

29

Jesus asks us to change in many ways. It takes commitment, patience, perseverance, and work to make the changes that are needed to become more like him.

A beautiful piece of prose that was given to me by a friend, and written by (deceased) Father Joseph Payne, CSC of Notre Dame University, captures the wonder of the possibilities of change for couples considering the vocation of marriage:

I am not who I was.
I am not going to be who I was going to be.
You changed all that.
You are not who you were.
You are not going to be who you were going to be.
I changed all that.

What is "Poor, and cannot not be.
What was "Poor, and cannot not have been.

So you see, my friend, we are us.

Who are we going to be?
We are going to be who we never could have been
Without each other.[16]

God has incredible gifts and graces for everyone. He patiently waits for us to receive them. One of those gifts might be a calling to a vocation in the Roman Catholic Church as a consecrated brother or sister, to serve the "suffering Christ." Or a man may be called to become an ordained deacon or priest. Or a lay person may be drawn to work in prison ministry.

Let God use us as his vessels of mercy to serve others. Let this be our purpose in life. What else could be a higher purpose than this? Years ago, I read *The Purpose Driven*

---

[16] "He Changed Our Lives: Rev. Joseph E. Payne, CSC, 1907-1976" by Dr. John E. Peck.

Life,[17] given to me by my friend, Marsha. I remember how fundamental and vital the message of this book was for me. At first, I wasn't interested in the book, then eventually finished it.

Knowing our purpose in life settles restless souls, and serving those in need will fulfill that purpose, especially when it is following God's Will for us.

Father Pedro Arrupe's prose suggests we find what breaks our hearts, then let that one thing motivate us every day. For example, it is important for practicing Christians to work to abolish the death penalty, abortion, human trafficking, and other *injustices against the dignity of life.*

Nothing Is More Practical Than Finding God[18]

Nothing is more practical than
finding God, than falling in love
in a quiet absolute, final way.

What you are in love with,
what seizes your imagination,
will affect everything.
It will decide
what will get you out of bed in the morning,
what you do with your evenings,
how you spend your weekends,
what you read, whom you know,
what breaks your heart,

---

[17] Rick Warren, *The Purpose Driven Life* (Grand Rapids, Michigan: Zondervan, 2002).

[18] From "Rooted and Grounded in Love: A Talk of Father Pedro Arrupe to the Participants in an Ignatian Course, and Later Addressed to All Jesuits" (Anand: Gujarat Sahitya Prakash, 1981).

and what amazes you with joy and gratitude.
Fall in Love, stay in love,
and it will decide everything.

Father Pedro Arrupe, SJ

We all have something in common on the subject of change. That is, we will experience many changes in our lives. We will have endless opportunities for change. Change can be refreshing, enriching, stimulating, adventurous, motivating, rewarding, and fulfilling.

We choose how to react to change.

Our faith in God can lead us to places we would never have dreamed of. All we need is faith the size of a mustard seed (Mt. 17:20).

This book will focus on what can happen when one middle-aged woman chooses to make drastic changes in her life, specifically, what followed after she said "yes" to the calling from Jesus Christ to become a sister, and to serve those who suffer.

In my later and more recent years, I have *let God* change me in significant ways.

I am grateful to live in the United States of America, a country where a person can still prosper by their own efforts, and with the grace of God. He has given me so much to be thankful for. I doubt I would have experienced so many changes in life had I lived in a third world country, or one that is under communist control.

Our country is still a democratic society of change for individuals with a strong work ethic, and for this, I am grateful. I am also most thankful for living in a country where we can still worship as we choose, and in public places, as our founding fathers first established for this country.

Anyone can change. A good friend once said to me, "I can do anything; I can't do everything." He meant we have far more potential than we realize. Of course, we cannot do everything there is to do in life, for that is physically impossible for one human being. The possibilities for one person, however, are endless. And with God, all things are possible, as long as it is consistent with his will for us. "Jesus looked at them and said, 'For human beings it is impossible, but not for God. All things are possible for God'" (Mk. 10:27).

The key to learning God's will for us is to stay in prayer and actively listen in the silence for what it is that God wants us to know and to do. In the Catholic faith tradition, one way to do this is to spend time in Eucharistic Adoration, where we sit quietly in the silence with Jesus Christ, who we believe is physically and substantially present in the Eucharist.[19]

Another way to pray is simply to remove all distractions in the home, light a candle, and be present for an hour, talking with God about the day. Invite Jesus into your heart to become your best friend, to have a personal relationship with him. Then be patient, waiting to hear what God wants to say to you. *Begin and end all efforts with prayer, and see how life changes for the better, and in very peaceful ways.*

Have you been tapped on the shoulder by God to consider serving those in need as a consecrated Catholic sister or brother, ordained deacon or priest? There is no better job and no better boss. God provides all the resources you will need. There is no greater joy; however, giving birth to my

---

[19] "By the consecration, the transubstantiation of the bread and wine into the Body and Blood of Christ is brought about. Under the consecrated species of bread and wine, Christ himself, living and glorious, is present in a true, real and substantial manner: His Body and Blood, with his soul and divinity." (CCC 1413; see also, Council of Trent: DS 1640, 1651).

three sons, loving them and raising them, was also joyful. Everything has its own time in life. My sons now have their own families and are experiencing the joy of their families. As a divorced Mom and empty-nester, God knew the best time to tap me on the shoulder to tell me to follow him.

Consider making drastic changes to serve as a *habited* sister or brother. Why? Many times, because of the habit and veil, I have been approached in public by strangers who have questions about many things. Wearing the habit and veil are outward signs of our commitment to consecrated life. They are signs of the Catholic Church, and signs of our Christian faith. There are also sisters of orders and other associations of the faithful who chose not to wear the habit and veil, and they serve joyfully as well.

The following is a story of what can happen when a sister wears a habit and veil in public.

A friend of mine told me that his friend saw me shopping in a department store one day. He said that when his friend saw me, he felt a sense of peace come over him, by merely seeing a Catholic sister in a religious habit and veil, and knowing we bring hope and peace to others. When my friend shared this with me, I then felt a sense of confirmation from God that I was doing what he called me to do, to serve others, and to provide Catholic witness to the world.

I am filled with joy knowing that a person's life can be positively impacted just by seeing a Catholic sister in a habit and veil. This happened because I committed to making drastic changes to my life. And I should interject here that in formation we are taught that we respect the habit. This means that we do not go ziplining or ride a motorcycle after we become consecrated sisters, wearing the habit and veil. Because our habits are blessed, they are sacred garments, and we respect them.

God sends us people who are seeking, and we help them, even if it is just listening to them for a few minutes. And these meetings happen every day. There is no appointment, no meeting place, no manager in charge. God simply arranges spontaneous meetings. I love how he works, and I can see his hand at work every time. *He orchestrates life as he sees fit, and on his schedule, not ours.*

The calling from Jesus in 2010 was probably the most pivotal time in my life. I did not see it coming. I had no idea that God would have had this in store for me, a great sinner. I thought I was not worthy of being a sister, of all things! How could he possibly want *me* to be a Catholic sister? This could not be correct. *He must have called the wrong woman.*

Anyone can choose to change, to follow Jesus. Anyone can leave themselves behind and follow him. It is a choice to follow him, and to make drastic changes to one's life. All of us are called to follow him though. We can follow him in different vocations, e.g., single life, married, or religious. Whatever route we take, we need to *let Jesus lead us through* the trials and tribulations of life.

Expect many changes along the way. And expect that you will continue to change as a person many times, and in many ways. A person can also choose to strive to change, to become more holy every day, although failing at times, which is human. We have to keep going, trusting God along the way.

Questions for the reader to contemplate: If I received a calling from Jesus to become a priest, deacon, sister or brother, or any other vocation, am I open to making drastic changes to my life, to serve others? What do I need to free myself of to follow Jesus? Spend some time in silent prayer to contemplate this.

CHAPTER 2
LIFE BEFORE THE CALLING

~>/|\~

This is a rather long chapter, because it represents who I was before I received the calling; however, God uses *all* of our former life experiences when we are called later in life.

Before Jesus called me to become a nun, my vocations were wife, United States Air Force airman, mother, businesswoman, and manager. Did I include Jesus in my daily challenges? Did I pray before I started a task or project, asking for help, guidance, and wisdom? Did I pray to give thanks to God afterward? Was I lost? Did I know what my purpose in life was during these vocations? Did I know God, Jesus, and Mary on a personal level?

I was born into a Roman Catholic family with devout practicing Irish Catholics, at Hamilton Air Force Base, California, near San Francisco. At the time I was born, I had two older sisters, Becky and Sue. In large families like ours, from the time we are born, [jokingly] we have a number. I am number three. Donna was born a year after me, and her first home was my first home, something we have in common. We moved to Eglin Air Force Base, where Dot was born. Then to Norfolk Naval Air Station, where Mike was born. I'm sure our mother was surprised when she learned that Dad's next assignment would be North Africa! We moved to Wheelus Air Force Base, Tripoli, Libya, Africa. Mom gave birth to three children in a four-year timeframe - Jimmy, Jackie, and

Bobby, during the time we lived there. Then we relocated to McGuire Air Force Base, New Jersey, where the youngest child, Mary, was born. We would move to three more bases before Dad retired; respectively, Richards-Gebaur Air Force Base, Missouri, Hickam Air Force Base, Hawaii, and Robins Air Force Base, Georgia.

Eleven children. One of our siblings, William, named after our father, died an hour after birth, from what we understand. At least Mom and Dad were able to spend time with him for that hour. I am sure the mercy of God prevailed over him as the angels welcomed him into heaven. All of us wish we had known him.

All of my remaining nine siblings and I were baptized shortly after birth. According to my baptismal certificate, I was baptized into the Catholic faith two weeks after birth, a standard practice at that time that still exists today. Today the church asks parents to take a course to learn about the Sacrament of Baptism and teaches the parents and godparents their responsibilities during the life of the child. Baptism is a Sacrament of Initiation into the Christian faith.[20]

While we lived in Tripoli, we learned Arabic in the Department of Defense schools on the base. We experienced massive sand storms, causing us to close all the windows and doors, and not go anywhere until they were over. We rode camels at the school carnival once a year. We also walked down the road from our villa[21] to swim in the Mediterranean Sea. Because of Dad's responsibility as Wing Commander, he and our mother were invited to have dinner with the Chief of Police for Libya, who at that time was the infamous Muammar Quadafi. I wish I could have seen our Iowan parents experience this event!

---

[20] CCC 1413
[21] We lived in an old villa that had been one of Italian fascist Benito Mussolini's resort homes at one time.

After relocating twenty-four times in my life—which included moves with my dad, then my husband, and relocations through my own employment—I was surprised to find that I still had some items in my hope chest from when I made my First Communion, Reconciliation, and Confirmation! After all those moves from one state or country to another, I still have the white lace veil, Catechism book, certificate, and rosary. Many times, I organized and packed these things and did not seem to notice them. After my calling from Jesus to become a nun, I *saw* them. *And suddenly, they were of great importance to me.*

All of us received the Sacraments of Initiation (Baptism, Reconciliation, First Communion, and Confirmation) when we were children, usually in the second grade, and all-at-once. Our parents instilled in us a firm foundation of faith as we were growing up. I fell away from the Church for some time after I was divorced, and returned to the Church later.

First Holy Communion
Catechism Book

First Holy Communion
Remembrance Card

First Holy Communion Veil   First Holy Communion Rosary

First Holy Communion Picture - 1962. First row, third from the left.

But no matter where I was in the world, I always felt at home when I walked into a Catholic church. This was true even if I was in a church of a foreign country and did not know the language! Why? Because the Eucharist was present, and the content of the Mass was still the same, no matter where I was.

When I was a child, the first time I felt tapped on the shoulder to become a nun was at fourteen years old. Many girls between the ages of twelve and fourteen still feel this calling. I know this from screening middle-aged women for the possibility of becoming candidates with our association of sisters.[22]

And what is interesting to me is that our Blessed Mother Mary, the mother of Jesus Christ, was around this age when the Angel Gabriel visited her to announce that she would have a child!

Once I was asked to be the May Queen at Sunday Mass, again at fourteen years old, to sit in a place of honor close to the altar of the church during Mass. I did not know what this was about at the time. I since learned the practice of the crowning of the May Queen is to honor Mary, the mother of Jesus Christ. She played an important role in our salvation through her fiat, her "yes" to the will of God, that she would become the mother of Jesus.

I wore a light pink A-line dress that day, with a beautiful white lace veil on my head fastened with a bobby pin, and white patent leather flats. I especially remember that I did not move the entire time during Mass as I was so frightened about sitting so close to the altar, and knowing that everyone was looking at me!

---

[22] Chapter six of this book is devoted to the Eudist Servants of The Eleventh Hour. To learn more about our association of sisters, visit: www.eudistservants. org.

Shortly after this time, I became much more interested in boys. The idea of becoming a nun was quickly forgotten.

During my senior year in high school, I began dating a student in my English class. The summer after my high school graduation, and at the age of seventeen years old, I accepted a proposal of marriage from a fellow graduate. After being engaged for two years, and we both completed some college, we married at the Robins Air Force Base chapel, in Warner Robins, Georgia. I was nineteen, and he was twenty. We had a Catholic wedding. The reception was at the Officer's Club.

Wedding Picture - 1974

I planned all the details for our wedding. My fiancé was Baptist, and after discussion with him, he said he wanted to become Catholic before the wedding, that he had always been interested in the Catholic faith. My father was his godfather and sponsored him into the Catholic Church.

At twenty and twenty-one years old, my new husband and I entered the United States Air Force together, at the lowest enlisted rank of Airman Basic (no stripes). Basic military training was six weeks at Lackland Air Force Base, San Antonio, Texas. Personnel technical school immediately followed this at Keesler Air Force Base, Biloxi, Mississippi. During basic training, my husband and I were not allowed to live together, because everyone was separated by gender, but we were allowed to cohabitate during personnel training. We rented a cheap apartment.

Air Force Basic Training with Dean (husband) – Enlisted – 1975

Air Force – Rank of Airman Basic - 1975

An old blue station wagon was our transportation. Later, I had my long auburn hair cut into a page-boy style to conform to the regulations for women, not to be longer than the shirt collar. And women weren't allowed to have ponytails. I learned this the first morning of training when an instructor yelled in my face that I would *not* have a ponytail the next time I saw him, and he loudly announced this in the presence of several hundred women in the chow hall!

Shorter hair was much easier to care for. The most liberating change, though, would come later after making vows as a Catholic sister, because I would choose to buzz off all my hair. No one would see it anyway under my cap and veil. This was a *choice of change* I looked forward to, and still enjoy.

After we completed our training, we applied for a joint assignment to the Pentagon, our first assignment, and highly unusual for the lowest ranking airmen we were. Initially though, he was assigned to Fairchild Air Force Base, Washington, and I was assigned to Wurtsmith Air Force Base, Michigan. We thought we were about to be separated; instead, we were approved for a joint assignment to the Pentagon.

A requirement was that the applicant must have a high graduation score to be accepted. He did, but I did not. We were concerned we would be assigned to two different locations; however, the Air Force made an exception for me because we were married. I was allowed to relocate with him as a joint assignment to the Air Force Consolidated Base Personnel Office of the Pentagon. We both began as record clerks, then gained experience in incoming and outbound military relocations of officers and enlisted personnel.

We enjoyed wearing uniforms every day, no longer having to shop much for civilian clothing and accessories. We cleaned and ironed our uniforms ourselves. I sewed the new stripes on all of our shirts each time we would advance in the ranks. One day as we were walking into the Pentagon shortly after we made a new rank, I noticed my husband's shirt did not have any stripes on one shirt sleeve. I accidentally left them off when I was changing the stripes on one of his shirts! He had to go home and change his shirt, then return to work, unfortunately. I felt terrible about that.

After three years and three months of service, I separated from the Air Force, due to pressure at that time for expectant active-duty mothers to separate from the service, rather than to remain on active duty. We were expecting our first child. I became a Veteran.

We relocated to Randolph Air Force Base, San Antonio, Texas, where my husband worked at the Air Force Personnel headquarters. He was accepted into the Bootstrap Commissioning program to attend college full-time to earn his bachelor's degree and to become an officer. I also returned to college, using the G.I. Bill as a Veteran, going to night school. Two years later we relocated to Bergstrom Air Force Base, to live closer to the University of Texas-Austin campus, so my husband could attend college there to earn his electrical engineering degree. At the same time, I attended Texas Lutheran College, Saint Edwards University, and San Marcos University to obtain the course credits for my degree. In 1983, we both completed our bachelor's degrees. My double degree was in accounting and financial management.

During this time, I also gave birth to our first two sons, Chris and Joey, who were twenty-one months apart in age. We arranged for the baptism of both sons as Catholics at the Randolph Air Force Base chapel, several weeks after birth.

At one time, both children were in diapers—cloth diapers with metal diaper pins and plastic pants! We could not afford a diaper service. What a chore this was!

My husband attended Officer Training School at Lackland Air Force Base, San Antonio, Texas, and upon completion, became an officer. While he was in training, our two sons and I stayed with my parents at their home in Warner Robins, Georgia. I threw a massive party for him after his commissioning as an officer. Soon afterward, all four of us traveled to his first assignment as an officer, to Wright-Patterson Air Force Base, Ohio.

About six months after we arrived in Ohio, the Air Force hired me for part-time work as an accountant because of my degree and Veteran status. Accepted into a fast-track accountant program, I began working full-time, and worked up to a civil service GS-11 rank, working in accounting, foreign military sales, and financial reconciliation of funds. *When I was promoted to a GS-9 rank, my oldest son, Chris, who was seven years old at the time, said, "Mommy, now do you get to clean the whole building?"* He had only seen me clean house and had not yet seen me work in an office setting. He did not know any better, and was very excited for me.

Our sons began to go to daycare as well. Knowing that my children would be with someone else during the day was the most challenging part of being a working parent. Finding good daycare was a challenge, especially in the 1980s. *Looking back, I wish I could have been content to stay at home with our children. The days our children are with us are numbered and fly by quickly.* Then suddenly they are adults and leave to make their own lives, decisions, and grow their own families. And this is the way it should be, seeing them grow into independent and self-sufficient adults. But as their mother, I still miss them.

We spent four years at Wright-Patterson, and during this time, our third son, Bobby, was born. He was baptized into the Catholic Church shortly after birth as well. He was born early, before his due date, because I promised his older brothers that I would till the dirt with a hoe to prepare a garden. This activity brought on early labor pains. It was *not* a choice to *not* follow through with this promise to my sons! I did not want to let them down as they were excited about planting a garden in the back yard.

Our next assignment was to return to the Pentagon. Hired into the Policy & Management Division of the Office of International Affairs of the Secretary of the Air Force,[23] I

---

[23] The Office of the Secretary of the Air Force is the highest office of the United States Air Force.

was the point of contact for the pricing of all inventory aircraft, missiles, and helicopters for sale to foreign countries. And I was the program manager of the dormant Iranian program, coordinating with the State Department, White House, and Congress on the Iranian and U.S. Claims at Den Hague (World Court), the Netherlands. I worked on this program after the United States Embassy takeover happened in Iran, when many of the embassy workers were taken hostage. The Iranians made financial claims against the Department of Defense, and our job was to defend the U.S. Government and to mitigate damages.

I progressed to the level of a GS-13 Civil Servant. I worked there for eight years in a very stressful and demanding job. It was one of the most interesting jobs I have ever had, because it was troubleshooting issues about items on contracts between the United States Air Force and eighty foreign countries. The work involved coordinating with other government agencies and offices, as well as other military departments, including the Army and Navy. Frequently, the contracts we worked on were multi-million-dollar agreements, and many times the approval process included the White House, Congress, and the State Department.

Air Force Civil Servant, Pentagon, GS-13, 1996
Going away luncheon at a restaurant.

During this time, when I was thirty-eight years old, I was working very hard at my job, running errands, cleaning the house, cooking dinner, serving as a Boy Scout Leader, and trying to be superwoman.

Many women were trying to break the glass ceiling in the 1970s and 1980s, while being mothers, and it was hard work. I was steadily wearing myself down physically, emotionally, mentally, and spiritually.

Then one day, I became very sick and did not get better for what seemed to be a long time. For an entire month, I had a cyclical fever that would run up to 103 degrees every day, then the temperature would break, and the fever would begin again, going back up to 103 degrees. I was not able to work. I drank Gatorade like it was going out of style to ensure I was taking in enough electrolytes. I had joint and muscle pain throughout my entire body and shooting pains in my arms and legs. I would lay in bed at night crying from the intense pain.

Imagine having fever and chills every day with an undetermined ending date. All joints, muscles, and tendons ache. All joints are swollen and red, and this includes ankles, hands, hips, knees, jaw, elbows, and shoulders. I could not turn my head because the neck pain was so intense. I had swelling behind the knees from excess fluid. I could not stand up straight when trying to stand or walk with a full gait, or try to straighten the legs or arms completely. I could not raise my arms entirely over my head. I did not have energy or strength. Walking up or down steps was painful. Overall mobility was reduced each day. Dressing was difficult. Putting on a jacket and turning on a shower faucet was almost impossible. Every jar could only be opened with a special tool, and I am thankful someone thought to invent it!

Some people *do not understand or believe* that a person could be in such extreme pain without seeing any evidence of the pain, like bleeding or broken bones. It is very real pain, even though it is not visible to others.

After a month of extreme suffering and not getting better, my husband and I went to the local military medical facility, Fort Belvoir Army Medical Center, Virginia, and I begged the doctor to admit me to the hospital. She admitted me, and I felt a sense of relief that someone might be able to diagnose and treat me. She ran many tests, and all were negative. I had night sweats and changed hospital gowns several times a night. After being hospitalized for a week, the fever finally broke and did not return, and I was so relieved. The final diagnosis that was added to my medical record was "fever of unknown origin."

During the time in the hospital, I thought I was going to die. I slept with the lights on the entire time. A chaplain came to pray with me. I do not recall what he said, but I was crying, so his words must have touched my heart in some way. He was probably trying to give me a sense of hope.

During times of COVID-19 at the hospitals, it was comforting to know there were spiritually-grounded medical staff who were willing to pray with patients, especially when they were not allowed to have visitors. My sister, Jackie, in her sacred calling as a nurse, is one of those prayer warriors. *Her patients are fortunate to have her.*

Once we damage ourselves, sometimes unknowingly, as I was doing by trying to be supermom and working in very demanding jobs without managing my stress, chronic diseases can surface, changing our lives.

God would have me draw upon this extreme suffering later when I became a chaplain at the Blairsville, Georgia hospital, visiting patients to pray with them, and to lift their spirits. I never would have known at the time of my worst agony, that God would use it to understand the pain of others later in my life.

Two months after release from the Fort Belvoir hospital, I still was not well. New blood work results tested positive for rheumatoid arthritis. The specific test is the "RA Factor." I was diagnosed with severe rheumatoid arthritis. Fibromyalgia had also begun. What I did not know at the time, and according to one of my doctors, was that the big problem with my physiology was that my auto-immune system was "confused" due to a mutated T-1 cell; my immune system was attacking my own body. He explained that this can happen if health is not managed well by being mindful of stress management, adequate sleep, drinking enough water, and exercising.

After I was divorced and living alone when the arthritis and fibromyalgia flared up, there was no one to help. I do not think I wanted to have help, though, because I did not want to be a burden to anyone. And I was thankful to have a full-time administrative job where I worked at a desk most of the day. I was required to use my mental faculties rather than physical strength to perform a task.

Many years later, around fifty years old, when I was still trying to manage these diseases, I was so ill that even with potent medicines, I was in extreme pain. I desperately wanted to be healed. Then God led me to a Catholic doctor who practiced Eastern *and* Western medicine. I met Jen through the priest at our church. She taught me how to better manage my health. She changed my diet, and in two months, I was off all medicines and lost two dress sizes! I was in remission, and not taking any medicines for either of these diseases. She asked me to stop eating dairy, meat, fish, caffeine, and to only drink water. She wanted to first cleanse my system by eliminating these foods and eat only salads for a while. Afterwards, she told me to introduce substitutions, such as almond milk, beans, lentils, and tofu.

If we treat our bodies well, our bodies will treat us well.

Rheumatoid arthritis is hereditary. It is in my DNA, and it could have presented itself with or without stress, but stress is typically a significant factor. Also, many people will have either rheumatoid arthritis or fibromyalgia, not both. *I have both, but both are in remission now, and have been for years.*

Although this wonderful doctor, now a good friend of mine, guided me to better health by changing what I ate, the one long-lasting remedy would come later from finding inner peace through ardent prayer, meditation, reflection, and letting go.

Stress management, which is essential to improving health, was accomplished in my life by developing a strong prayer life to bring me to a place of peace. I could not have gotten to this point without God's grace. He led me out of a pit of despair of horrible, extreme suffering.

God uses me today to spot those who are "in the pit," just as I had been. I am drawn to them. I console them, because I know their pain.

It was at this time that I was drawn back to the Catholic Church. It was comforting to me. I started going to Sunday Mass, becoming re-acquainted with my faith, and receiving the Eucharist (Jesus Christ), who strengthened me. At one point later, I also attended the Rite of Christian Initiation of Adults (RCIA) classes in the evening to refresh myself in the faith.

Since the beginning of these illnesses, my auto-immune system attacked different areas of my body repeatedly: musculoskeletal (bones and muscles), thyroid, ovaries, musculoskeletal again, thyroid again, and musculoskeletal again. One area would go into remission, and I would be well for a short time, then another area would be adversely affected.

Unknowingly at first, I let my out-of-control stress control my health. Do you know that because of this, I now teach inmates breathing exercises, and also how to pray the Rosary, when the opportunity presents itself. And some prisoners are open to learn.

As of today, I am on maintenance medicines for aging conditions that many older people have - asthma, hypertension, cholesterol and heart rate, but not for rheumatoid arthritis or fibromyalgia. The inner peace I have now through my Catholic faith practices has caused me to enjoy a healthier and more mobile lifestyle.

God also spared me from permanent deformity of my joints. My formation house mother said she believed it was a miracle that I was no longer tormented from these diseases, and not taking medicines for them. Usually, a person with active rheumatoid arthritis would have hands with visible knots at the joints and red, swollen areas. I no longer have any swelling, red areas, or knots. My hands look entirely normal, other than the wrinkles of a sixty-five-year-old woman.

This next statement is very important. *At one point in my journey of great physical suffering, I told God in ardent prayer that, "I will do whatever you want for the rest of my life if you will just take away these diseases." He did. And I am doing what he wants now. He tells me what to do, and I am doing it. I am doing his will, not mine. God and I have a pact.* We understand each other. He knows I am serious and committed.

He will use every gift he has given me in life, to serve others as he desires, whether that is a Saint Vincent de Paul Society home visit, visiting a death row inmate, consoling someone in an airport or grocery store, helping a prisoner find answers to their questions about God and their purpose in life, working to abolish the death penalty in Georgia, helping others to start prison ministry programs, or developing formation material to help Saint Vincent de Paul Society Vincentians with their spiritual growth, for example.

And finally, in 2008, I attended a three-day healing mission at Christ the King Cathedral in Atlanta, Georgia. I talk about this in depth in the next chapter when I share about the calling to become a sister. I asked God to heal me physically, and this is when he began my spiritual healing first, before the physical healing began, which came about through prayer and finding inner peace.

Continuing to share about this journey of life before the calling, after we had been at the Pentagon for six years, my husband received orders to report to Griffiss Air Force Base, New York, for a two-year assignment. This service would complete his twenty years, then he could retire from the Air Force.

I was about to make the worst decision of my life. I was tired of relocating from one place to another, I had an excellent job, the children had their friends and did not want to move, and all of them were established in Boy Scouts. My husband and I were also Boy Scout leaders at the time.

I made the selfish decision of choosing not to relocate our sons and myself to accompany my husband to New York. I reasoned that it was only two years, and at the end of this time, our family would reunite. This decision was a significant contributor to the beginning of the break-up of our marriage.

During these last two years of service, while we were living apart, I was responsible for everything. There were no longer any shared duties of raising the children and responsibilities of the home. These were the consequences of the decision that I had to endure.

Additionally, I became depressed after he left, to the point of having to be on anti-depressant medicine for three months. Eventually, I did not like feeling flat from the medicine, not laughing or crying, and took myself off the medication. It was a temporary crutch that I needed, because before I was on the medicine, during the time I was separated, I was constantly crying.

And it was also at a time when I did not know Jesus, nor did I know how to pray ardently. He was not at the center of anything in my life, or the lives of my family. We still went to Mass every Sunday, but that was the extent of my connection to God. Since that time, I have witnessed happy, healthy families whose center is Jesus, and the difference is remarkable when they adapt his teachings to their lives.

At the end of the two years, he retired, and we all eventually relocated to Roswell, Georgia. Soon after that, we divorced. The saddest part of a divorce is the outcome for the children and how painful it is for them. It is difficult for the husband and wife, but more hurtful for the children. *I know both of us were very sorry for this. This is a part of our lives I wish had never happened.* Our oldest son went to college, and our other sons lived with me, with joint custody.

I believe that our grown sons are the dedicated, loyal fathers they are today, because of the separation and divorce they witnessed of my husband and me. I am incredibly proud of my sons and daughters-in-law as spouses and parents.

The few times we gather every year are very special. We enjoy each other's company and have a lot of laughs together. I especially enjoy watching the grandchildren play, because they remind me so much of our sons when they were younger. And I love being a grandmother to them, watching them grow, laugh, and play.

At the new Georgia location, I could not find employment initially with my government experience. I finally accepted a job through a temporary agency to work as an administrative assistant in a corporate office. Shortly after that, I was hired as a contract supervisor. Four years later, I was supervising ten employees on the administration of contracts to allow the company to buy and sell excess power, gas, and other derivatives, with energy companies.

I eventually thought it was time for me to be my own boss, so I resigned from the company to become a real estate agent. When I left the company, I told the personnel manager that the only difference between military and corporate is that the military is all on the same page, working towards the same goal; while, what I saw in the corporate world was that everyone seems to have a different agenda. I was uncomfortable with the corporate environment because of this, at least in my own experience.

Atlanta Realtor - 2002

Being my own boss as an agent first required training and earning my state real estate license. During the next four years, I worked as an agent in the Atlanta metro area. It was arduous work with minimal payoff. I was only paid when the client's purchase or sale went to closing. The best result I had in real estate was selling five houses in two months and earning $20,000 in commission. The worst time I had as an agent was when I was sick, could not work, and had no income for six months. We lived off my credit cards and ate a lot of pork-n-beans! It was a difficult time.

This particular experience prepared me for working with the poor through the Saint Vincent de Paul Society. I have compassion for people who struggle financially, because I was in their shoes at one time.

It was during this time I acknowledged that I should go back to work for the federal government because I already had fifteen years of service and the benefits were excellent. I applied for positions in a lot of agencies and was hired for a federal civil service position.

Based upon my previous experience in policy and management at the GS-13 level, I was later promoted from a GS-7 to a GS-13. I then interviewed for the Chief position, GS-14, and was selected for the position. The responsibilities of this job were managing an office of fifty people, hiring/firing, counseling, documenting, conducting meetings, overseeing commercial printing equipment, complying with government regulations and audits, and decision making. There were many difficult challenges.

Typically, I worked more than the required eight hours a day. Some days I was authorized overtime by my supervisor, but there were many days I was not paid for overtime, due to a lack of funds. People say, "Oh the government, they don't work!" That could be, but I was never in a government job where I did not work long hours! There

Civil Service Federal Manager – 2008

was always plenty of work to do and never enough people to do it.

While I was working at the last agency I was employed at, a co-worker befriended me. Marsha was the only person who cared to become a friend when I started working there. Then she saw that I was *not* a Christ-centered person. I was lost. She was the person who gave me *The Purpose Driven Life*.[24] This book started me thinking about what my true purpose in life was.

Many years later, I learned my purpose in life was to serve the suffering Christ, whoever that might be. In fact, now I believe this is meant to be everyone's purpose in life.

Another good friend, Babi, saw that I was *not* centered in the Word of God, the Bible. She knew I was lost. She tried to talk to me about how important Jesus Christ is in our lives, but her message fell on deaf ears because I was not ready to hear this yet. I was not open to this at that time. Of course, I believed in God and Jesus Christ, but I did not have a personal relationship with him.

Another good friend and medical doctor, Jen, shared her Catholic faith with me during doctor appointments with her. She would tell me she saw a bright light within me. But I was still spiritually lost. *Now I pay others this kind compliment when I see it within them, shining through to me.* I mention Jen in another part of this book too, as she and her boyfriend witnessed an unexplained mystical phenomenon with me on one Christmas Eve night.

Another co-worker and Christian friend, Diana, also helped me along the way. Educated with a Doctorate in Theology, she coached me in the ways of God. At times I was not open to receive this guidance as my mind was

---

[24] Rick Warren, *The Purpose Driven Life* (Grand Rapids, Michigan: Zondervan, 2002).

occupied with work issues. She persevered to reach me when opportunities would arise. She was an important part of my journey as well. But at that time, I still remained lost.

Yet another Christian co-worker and friend, Shaun, showed me the light of Jesus in the workplace. He was a hard worker, slow to anger, always had a smile on his face, and devoted to his wife and family. He would also try to help me see the brighter side of life through his faith in Jesus. He knew as well that I was lost.

And my supervisor, Scott, presented himself as a person of great integrity, and strong Christian faith, another example for me to follow. He always identified the good in people during our office discussions, showing me a more positive outlook on life, and also became a source of spiritual support when it was needed.

I was not aware of the gifts God was placing all around me, of his devout practicing Christians, to be faith-filled examples for me to follow.

All of these spiritually-grounded people were placed on my path by God for a reason, to get my attention. For this, I am eternally grateful to all of them. There have been many other people who God put in my life who were good role models and inspirational people, including my very devout Catholic parents, my husband's parents, and my Aunt Patsy Powers, who is a dear soul to me.

At this point, I was drawing closer to become a sister, although I did not realize this was happening at the time. Also, Jesus had not yet called me. However, I was noticing that God was surrounding me with these beautiful, light-filled, genuine Christians, all who wanted more for me in life. It was very noticeable.

They all wanted me to know the unconditional love of God. They were trying to share with me their own inner peace that I so desperately needed myself. Finding inner peace is a gradual process that takes time.

As I drew closer to God, Jesus, and Mary, and to all that is good, I also noticed I was moving away from all that was evil.

There is a process one must go through to transition into a spiritually-based life, centered on pleasing God, and one that is not self-serving. Instead, the genuine practicing Christian serves others who are in need.

Jesus Christ gave us the best example when he allowed himself to be crucified on the cross for our sins, giving us that second chance at eternal life in heaven with him, God, Mary, all the angels and saints, and all those who have gone before us.

Spiritual warfare between the evil one and God takes place every day. We are tempted by the evil one to do his bidding for him on earth. *We choose* if we will allow ourselves to fall for his temptations to commit sins against God. If we agree to sin, this is displeasing to God.

I do not think it is necessary to list my sins here. My sins are between God and me. I *was*, what I would consider today, to have been a great sinner in my former life, before I became a Catholic sister. I made wrong choices. We are all accountable for our sins. I was grateful to be able to confess my sins to a Catholic priest and receive absolution, as long as I was very sorry for my sins. I wish these sins never would have happened, but they did. *They are my past now.*

What is sin? Sin is an offense against God. Sin offends God. *Sin distances us from God.* In prison ministry, when inmates are open to learning, we teach them how to process their old baggage (some of which can be their sins) so they can move past this time in their lives, regardless of whether they remain incarcerated, or are released.

Prisoners must serve their sentences for their crimes; additionally, they must identify the changes they need to make to become better versions of themselves, more holy in the eyes of God, and a better person.

It is the same for us on the outside of prison, that when we sin, we need to identify the changes we need to make to become better people, and more holy in the eyes of God, too.

Sin pleases Satan, the enemy of humanity. Every time we choose to sin against God, we entertain the evil one, who is always present.

There is a spiritual maturation of the human being, a realization that there is a higher power who can provide mercy and forgiveness to everyone who desires these things, that there is the hope of being reunited with loved ones in heaven after our physical death on earth.

We can choose, through our actions, that our lives will end physically at the grave with our souls going to hell; or, we can choose, through our actions, that our souls will go to purgatory, then to heaven, to be reunited with all of our family members who have died. I choose the latter.

I do not want my story to end six feet underground in a dark, cold pit. I am joyful, knowing there is the hope of being reunited with my mother, father, sister, and all my other relatives, as long as I continue to strive to become more holy every day, to avoid hell. Our stay here on earth is as short as the blink of an eye, relative to all space and time as we know it. I choose to be with all my family for eternity in heaven. I pray every single day that we will all be together.

During prison ministry one night at a detention center, a young woman who thought she was atheist said she did not believe in God, and that she was not sure that God existed. One of our team members, Lisa, asked if she believed that the devil exists. She said yes. We then both said that there must, therefore, be a God. Since that time, she has chosen to inquire more about the Christian faith, and became surrounded by other Christian inmates, helping her with her faith journey.

Blaise Pascal, famous French mathematician, inventor, Catholic theologian, and writer, has a simple, yet comical, way of looking at blind faith. "If I believe in God and life after death, and you do not, and if there is no God, we both lose when we die. However, if there is a God, you still lose, and I gain everything."[25]

This prisoner had a mustard seed-size of faith that God exists, and showed spiritual growth every time we met with her. She had hope of growing in the Christian faith. *She had spiritually-grounded, devout Christians in the detention center, helping her on the journey. She was open to learning more about Christianity and what it offers. She then had a sense of hope.*

What is most important is that we give all glory to a merciful God who forgives sins, that our sins are in the past, and that we do not repeat them. After we are absolved (forgiven) of our sins in confession with a Catholic priest, we pray:

Act of Contrition

Oh my God, I am heartily sorry for having offended thee, and I detest all my sins because I dread the loss of heaven and the pains of hell, but most of all, because I have offended thee, my God, who are all good and deserving of all my love. I firmly resolve, with the help of thy grace, to confess my sins, to do penance and to amend my life.

Amen

---

[25] Blaise Pascal, *Pensées*, trans. Roger Ariew (Indianapolis, Indiana: Hacket Publishing Company, 2004), 212-213.

The part some Catholics forget after their confession to a priest is the very last part of the prayer, "amend my life." If the person is *unwilling to make changes* to become more holy and to resist temptation and sin, then the person is not able to move towards the inner peace and fulfillment that awaits him.

God does not measure sin. We are all worthy of his forgiveness, no matter how grievous the sin is. And this applies to criminals who commit heinous crimes as well. One night at a detention center, a young female inmate asked, "Did you say that God doesn't measure how big my sins are?" I reiterated that he does not measure, then I said, "What would be the point of measuring if he forgives *all* sins, for which we are genuinely sorry?"

The most challenging type of forgiveness is forgiving ourselves. We can forgive others and ask for forgiveness in turn, but when it comes to forgiving ourselves, this can be a challenge. It can be done though.

If you have not had forgiveness talks yet with those you have offended, or who have offended you, please make an effort to do this. It is as essential for you, as it is for the person who hurt you. If you cannot bring yourself to speak with them directly, write them a letter asking forgiveness or giving forgiveness, whichever applies. This is a liberating exercise and one that I recommend to others frequently.

One day I called my ex-husband and said, "You know, we have not had forgiveness talks yet. We need to do that. I am very sorry for what I have done, and I hope you are sorry for what you have done. I hope we can forgive each other. I forgive you; can you forgive me too?" We then said that we forgave each other. This was a big step for us that took place many years after the divorce. It was important to work towards renewed peace among our family members, even though we were divorced.

Someone has to take the first step in asking for, or granting, forgiveness. Someone has to have the courage to humble themselves, even at the risk of being hurt again. I was relieved that my ex-husband and I began to have amicable discussions with one another after these talks.

One of my fellow religious sisters told me during my formation, "Nobody wants to see it, smell it or look at it. It stinks. Throw it out." She was referring to the "garbage" she called it, that we carry around with us. If we rid ourselves of our old baggage, and make room for the Holy Spirit of God, we can be open to see what he has waiting for us. Holding a grudge against someone is unhealthy. Let it go and let the Holy Spirit of God enter our lives. *He has prepared something for each of us.*

Know that every human being sins against God. With God, all sins can be overcome with prayer, forgiveness, and if you are Catholic, absolved of your sins through the Sacrament of Reconciliation. In this way, we start again with a clean slate, and we are reminded when we pray the Act of Contrition prayer that we promise to amend our lives going forward. That means that it is *not okay* to commit a sin, confess it, be absolved of it, then think that it is okay to commit the same sin again. That is not how it works!

We should always strive to change our lives to become more holy by *not* committing the same sins over and over.

God uses every bit of my former life experiences for his purposes today, in my new life as a consecrated Catholic sister.

Questions for the reader to contemplate: Can I see how God can lead me out of the darkness? Where am I on my journey of faith? Am I doing the work necessary to cleanse my soul of past sins, and to resist temptation to sin? Is God using my physical, mental, spiritual, and emotional suffering experiences to become more compassionate, to serve those who suffer around me? What does God have waiting for me? Am I willing to sit in the silence to develop a personal relationship with Jesus, to become my best friend?

CHAPTER 3
THE CALLING, PRAYER, AND DISCERNMENT

Iconfess my sins to a Roman Catholic priest with genuine sorrow, and he absolves me under his authority as a priest, through the Sacrament of Reconciliation. It is as though Jesus himself is sitting with me, consoling me through my sorrow and failings, and lifting me up with his reassuring words of mercy and forgiveness.

Jesus lifted up Saul too. My journey was like that of Saul, who became Saint Paul. Saul was a great sinner. Although I was not persecuting the church as Saul was, I offended God with my sins as well.

"Now as he (Saul) journeyed he approached Damascus, and suddenly a light from heaven flashed about him and he fell to the ground and heard a voice saying to him, 'Saul, Saul, why do you persecute me? And he said, 'Who are you, Lord?' And he said, 'I am Jesus, whom you are persecuting; but rise and enter the city, and you will be told what you are to do" (Acts. 9:3-6).

Like Saul, he had to knock me off my high horse to get my attention. I was spiritually blind *before* God got my attention. And as with Saul, Jesus then told me what to do. I obeyed him because I knew he was the only beloved son of God, my maker, the one who should receive all glory and praise. I heard his voice for two years before I received the calling, a voice of only good and positive things.

I was selfish, self-centered, and so career-driven that I could not see straight; however, I was still, and always will be, a mother who dearly loves her sons and their families, which is fulfilling and joyful, yet I was also driven to excel in my career. My sons were grown at the time of the calling, and I was an empty nester.

Being a successful career woman, in my view, was not fulfilling or joyful. I can attest to this truth now because before the calling and before I retired, I had an excellent income with great benefits. *I worked up to a high level in government only to find that this was not the fulfillment of my life's purpose.*

One more promotion, pay raise, career, did not provide me with the fulfillment and joy I now have as a Catholic sister who serves the least of my brothers and sisters. At the time I worked in these careers—all administrative positions—it was my perception at that time that I was fulfilled and joyful in my life. *Knowing what I know now, comparing those careers to the ministries I do now, I am grateful that I can see the difference.*

Jesus Christ said, "Those who are well do not need a physician, but the sick do. I did not come to call the righteous but sinners" (Mk. 2:13-17). I now know that Jesus feels this way about me. This is probably why he has such a large following of believers too!

Numerous significant unexplained events happened to me before and after the calling from Jesus to become a sister. For now, I will focus on the events that occurred before the calling.

In March 2008, the first significant event of healing happened, although when it was over, I did not see any recognizable difference in the swelling of my hands, and I will explain this later in the story. I attended a three-day charismatic healing mission given by a visiting Philippines priest at the Christ the King Cathedral, Atlanta, Georgia. Yes, the Catholic Church has charismatic healing services! This priest had the gift of healing since the time he was a teenager. I saw the announcement of the mission in the church bulletin, thinking that this priest may be able to heal me of my rheumatoid arthritis and fibromyalgia. I was leading a stressful life in my career, which caused these diseases to be excruciatingly painful. I wanted so much to heal, and God knew this about me.

On the first night of the mission, the priest celebrated Mass and recited a healing prayer for the entire body, from head to toe, asking us to place our hands over the areas of pain in our bodies. For me, that meant crossing my arms over my chest, because I hurt all over my body and was in extreme pain. Everyone who wanted to, could also confess their sins to a priest that night. And so, I did.

On the second night of the mission, the priest recited the healing prayer again. Then we were all invited to go to the Communion rail, close to the altar, to wait for the priest to pray over us, one at a time. When the priest came to the woman next to me, to pray over her, she fell to the floor. Catchers were available to make sure people would not get hurt when they fell. I had never seen this and watched in awe as other people were also falling, not moving, some making sounds, some crying, one woman wailing through her tears. I stood there, not knowing what to expect as I had never seen "being slain in the spirit" or "resting in the spirit" in the Catholic Church.

I wanted so much to be healed of my pain. I learned later that when God heals a person, typically it is from the inside out. We have to work at processing our old baggage, to make room for the Holy Spirit of God. We must rid ourselves of that which is not of God, to be able to receive the Holy Spirit of God. And it takes work and a daily commitment on our part to change our bad habits and rid ourselves of things that are not of God, things that offend him.

Walking back to the pew, I felt as though nothing had happened, when in fact, God heard my prayer to be healed, and he had already begun to work on my healing, starting with the new Christian friends he had surrounded me with. He had also drawn me to this three-day healing mission.

The next day I shared the experience of the second night of the mission with one of my Christian friends at work, who expressed an interest in going with me on the third night. The priest gave the parishioners the healing prayer again, then invited us to join him at the Communion rail for individual healing. At this point, I desired God's healing touch to such a degree that I broke down in tears, waiting for the priest to heal me while I stood at the rail. I was yearning for good health and wellness and especially inner peace. I did not realize at the time that it would be a journey, and that immediate healing does not usually happen.

A catcher placed me directly in front of one of the most beautiful Crucifixes I have ever seen, all white marble and golden mosaic tiles. Jesus seemed larger than life to me as I stood, once again, waiting for the healing priest to cure me.

Then something happened that is unexplainable. *I could not move.* I cried uncontrollably and was shaking all over. I knew people were falling around me, they were coming and going, but I could not move. The friend who attended the mission with me, accompanied me to the Communion rail for healing as well. She left the Communion rail before me. The priest already stopped to give me his blessing, to pray over me, then moved on to another person. *I still could not move.* I wanted to, but I was frozen. It was as though my entire being said that I was not going anywhere until this priest cured me!

We were told not to speak to the priest, that he already knows where our pain is. That is true, because when he prayed over me, he placed his hand on my upper chest, knowing exactly where I had put my hands when he recited the healing prayer earlier in the evening! How did he know where I had placed my hands earlier in the service when he prayed the healing prayer for all the parishioners? He must have had the gift of healing because I did not tell him where the pain was!

Crucifix of Christ the King Cathedral, Atlanta, GA - 2008

The priest must have noticed that I was still standing there, crying uncontrollably and shaking. He came back to me. My eyes were still closed, but I knew he was there. He usually prays over a person only once, but he was about to pray over me for the second time. This time he placed his hands on my shoulders and prayed over me. Then most unexpectedly, he pushed my forehead back with the palm of his hand. I still did not fall. Even with a firm push from this healing priest, I remained solidly standing in place.

Everyone who knows anything about charismatic healing will tell you that you do not have to fall to the floor to receive the Holy Spirit of God, yet I yearned to let go and fall. I wanted to *rest* in the Holy Spirit of God. I was stubborn and prideful. *This was a conflict of my heart, mind, and soul.*

Since that time, I have rested in the spirit, in charismatic healing services in the Catholic Church, seven times. Every time it feels as though I am as light as a feather when I collapse to the floor and rest in the Holy Spirit of God. A warming sensation flows through my entire body.

Soon after the priest attempted to help me rest in the spirit, I was finally able to move, and I walked away from the altar, towards the friend who came with me. She could see that I was weak and trembling, and she held on to my arm to hold me up. While we walked towards our pew, the monsignor of the church asked me, in a very concerned way, "Are you healed, are you healed?" I said, in a desperate way, "I don't know, I don't know!" My friend said in a stern voice, "Oh, she's healed." She and I still laugh about that.

Unbeknownst to me at the time, God began to heal me from the inside.

We decided to sit in the very last pew of the church because I said that I did not want to leave. I wanted to continue to experience the evening by watching others go up to the Communion rail, thirty people across at a time, many falling and resting in the spirit, many just walking away. Several thousand people attended the three-day healing mission that night.

And I was still feeling the effects of the priest's healing, physically, mentally, spiritually, and emotionally, while we sat in that back pew. For a while I referred to this as my "spiritual explosion."

A significant statement was made by the priest earlier that night, *"If you did not fall down last night, do not blame me; it is probably that you have not forgiven someone."* While my friend and I sat in the back of the church, we both reflected on this question, "How many people have hurt me who I have not yet forgiven?" We both thought there were many on the list.

You see, there is work involved in becoming well, more holy, and more at peace with oneself.

While we sat in the back of the church, I kept looking at my hands to see if the swelling and red, hot joints had changed. No change. I checked over and over that night, and the next morning, to see if anything had changed physically. Nothing changed physically that I could see with my own eyes. I wanted an instant cure. I did not know at the time that God does not always work that way. I had to wait. I had to persevere.

That night my friend said, "Welcome Jesus into your heart." And so, I did, with all of my being, I invited him into my heart.

Spiritual healing began. I was unaware at the time that this was the beginning of my spiritual growth, and eventually finding inner peace through centered prayer. In time, my diseases went into complete remission, without potent medicines. This did not happen overnight.

Several spiritually-grounded people in my life from the Baptist faith and other Christian religions, seeing my suffering and need for healing, suggested that I welcome Jesus into my heart. *I always believed in God as the higher power, but I did not welcome him until I was fifty-three years old at this healing service.*

For the non-Christian reader, the Holy Trinity is a mystery of how God the Father, God the Son, and God the

Holy Spirit are three persons, yet one God, and this is the central mystery of the Christian faith and life.[26]

Two months after I welcomed Jesus, yearning for him to be with me, I began to hear a voice (not audibly) of goodness, hearing only good things, and nothing negative. This was new to me since most of my life I had been a negative person. There was no possible reason to begin to hear such good things, a conscience of goodness, from nowhere. How and why could this have happened so suddenly?

I was a woman of reason and logic, an educated career woman, and not under any more stress than most of my life had been, so why was this suddenly happening to me? Where was this voice coming from all of a sudden? And why was I hearing all these good things? What changed in my life?

I was turning to God, welcoming Jesus, opening myself to receive him. I was baptized into the Catholic faith marked with the sign of faith, two weeks after I was born.[27] Somehow along the way of life, though, I left my faith behind.

In May 2008, several months after the healing mission, I made the difficult decision to relocate to a new work location in another state, to work the last few years of my career, and become eligible for retirement. In doing so, I would have to live and work there without any family living near me.

I found myself completely alone for the first time in my life. This would become another turning point on my journey.

During this time, I relocated my office from Atlanta to the new location. I was having my new house built at the same time, and I lived in a hotel for three months while the builder finished the house. It was a dream. It was a house with three levels, even a finished basement, for one person

---

[26] CCC 232-237
[27] CCC 1231

to live. *Just me.* Why did I buy this much square footage? For my sons and their families to be comfortable when they visited me. I was thinking of how nice it will be when we are all together at my home.

After I moved into the house, the novelty of a new home wore off, and I began to see that I was utterly alone. The house was void of other human beings. No family or friends lived near me. *I found myself in the silence. Later I realized God put me on a sabbatical during this time. I was unaware of what he was doing. You see, this was another step in God's design for me. He works with us one step at a time.*

My favorite scripture is Psalm 46:10, "Be still and know that I am God." He had to get my attention because I was lost. During this sabbatical, and in the silence, I began to hear the voice—it was the voice of Jesus Christ, even though I did not know it at the time.

Out of the silence came the desire to return to a place of comfort – the Church. I was being drawn back to the Church, the Catholic Church, my Church. It is the only place I know I can go anywhere in the world, and know that I am home, and not alone. It is a place that is familiar to me no matter where I go, and that is comforting to know. I began to find my way to inner peace, one day at a time, one Mass at a time, one homily at a time. And I swear each homily was meant only for me when the priest was speaking! Has that happened to you?

Silence also caused me to contemplate the idea of taking Jesus to work with me, praying at work, talking things over with Jesus before I began work, and thanking him for helping me with the work. Once I started this practice, my life got to be a lot easier. Making decisions came easy. The stress was gone. Rheumatoid arthritis and fibromyalgia were in remission, and I was no longer taking any medicines for these diseases.

I like to share with others that when I tried to accomplish something without God, the results were 86%, but *with* Jesus, they were 110% every time.[28] Not only does he provide, but he gives us so much more than we could ever expect, if we just let him take over after we have used our own resources first, letting go of the rest to surrender to him. "The rest" can be too much for us without his help. Trusting him along the way is critical.

I also started to go to weekend retreats. These were powerful, spiritual experiences that helped me to grow much more deeply in spiritual ways, understanding more about what a relationship with Jesus Christ truly is.

Another special part of my spiritual growth came about through missionary work in Jamaica with Food for the Poor, Inc., during April 17-25, 2009. This mission trip took place one year after I began to hear the voice of Jesus, and one year before he gave me the calling to become a Catholic sister.

Are you beginning to see how God worked with me, one step at a time?

Father Tony Palazzolo was the speaker with Food for the Poor Inc., who celebrated Mass at the Catholic church I attended, and he spoke of the terrible conditions in the poor areas of Jamaica. He invited the parishioners to join him on a mission trip. *I had no plan to do this.* After Mass, I was drawn to a table that had information on the mission trip. For whatever reason, I asked the silliest question of a woman who had previously been on a mission trip with this priest. I said, "So I suppose you don't wear makeup when you go on these trips?" She said, "No, but I usually take my hairdryer." I

---

[28] Of course, these random percentages are used here only to help demonstrate how much better work results can be when our faith is present in our work throughout the day.

asked her several questions, and I told her I did not know if I could do this. She told me to pray about it.

While I was talking with the missionary at the table, Father Tony came over, extended his hand to me, and said, "Come to Jamaica with me." I said, "Don't tempt me!" Later that day, *I talked with Jesus about this in prayer, and I learned that I had absolutely no reason not to go.* I called to tell him that I did not think I was qualified, but that I would go.

You see, we cannot question or doubt God's plans for us. He knows what he is doing; we do not. We think we know, using our human intuition, logic, reason, and knowledge. The longer I am on this journey with him, the more I see his hand at work every day, and have come to trust him and his ways in all things.

When he calls us, *he will also give us his grace* to help us become qualified to do whatever it is he is calling us to do. This mission trip gave God the opportunity to show me many things in life I had not yet seen about others, especially the least of my brothers and sisters, and about myself. *With this trip, my eyes were opened. My heart began to soften.*

The first stop of this mission trip was at the Food for the Poor, Inc. headquarters in Florida. When we entered the building, we all walked right past a statue at the entrance. *We did not notice that it was a sculpture of a huddled mass on the floor. It was a homeless person. It was a sculpture of Jesus, the suffering Christ.* We had to get down on bended knee, literally humbling ourselves, to be able to peer up into the face that was shrouded in cloth, to see him.

Jesus, the suffering Christ.

Everyone on this mission trip took a moment to go back to the statue to bend down far enough to look up into the face of this statue. *This experience awakened me to actively look for those who suffer; whereas, previously, I would stay focused on wherever I was going at the moment, not noticing the least of our brothers and sisters. I was so busy with life that I didn't stop to notice them.*

Part of the trip took us to the mountains of Mandeville, Jamaica, to a boys' orphanage. The boys were abandoned by their families, most left in Montego Bay to commit petty crimes to earn a way of life, then arrested and brought to the orphanage. The orphanage was established by Saint John Bosco and was run by the Sisters of Mercy.

Jamaica Mission Trip - St. John Bosco Boys Orphanage - 2009

While we stayed at the orphanage, we were invited to witness the slaughter of chickens and pigs. I declined. I am always the one with the weak knees and a history of fainting! No, thank you. These young boys, though, learn the art of butchery at the orphanage, then take their skills to places of work to earn a living. There were other skills and trades available for them to learn as well.

On Sunday, Mass was celebrated by the bishop and a priest in Mandeville. During the homily, the bishop said to us, "He (Jesus Christ) is showing us his wounds. It is the message he gives to us."

This is the message that completed the mystery and answered for me, the question of "How does your dying on the cross and dying for our sins have anything to do with me?" He said in the homily, "Whatsoever you do to the least of my brothers, that you do unto me" (Mt. 25:40). This means that if we turn our backs on the poor, we turn our backs on Jesus. I had certainly done that in my life. It was not purposeful; it was just that I was so busy being a wife, mother, and career woman, that I did not seem to have time for anything else.

On the wall close to the altar is a sign, "By his stripes, we are healed" (Is. 53:45). Coincidentally, I had already seen this scripture reference several times before this mission trip, but it did not resonate with me until that trip.

God was trying so hard to get my attention. He was telling me I am finally healed through the pain and suffering of Jesus Christ. That message was for me that day. I was beginning to feel inner peace, liberation from my past sins against God, and finally starting to forgive myself and others. I was finding freedom in God's illogical ways.

By the way, as practicing and faithful Christians, we do not believe in coincidences at all. God is in charge. Look for this. If we are open to seeing this, we will see how everything is connected. For example, I believe the only reason some people are wealthy is to allow them the opportunity to share their blessings with the less advantaged. This is how God's Providence works.

We are all connected in some way, and through these connections and service to others, we find our true purpose in life.

We also visited a Mustard Seed Community of children who have special needs and have been abandoned by their families. I brought along with me a marionette (puppet) that my husband and I purchased for our youngest son, Bobby, when he was five years old. There was a reason I had kept this marionette named Charlie all those years through all the relocations I had, and finally, I knew why. The children were so excited to see Charlie dancing, playing, and even napping.

Charlie went with us to a place of abandoned girls, Glenhope Place of Safety. The girls had Jamaican music playing on the CD player, and we were all dancing in the courtyard. What surprised me, though, was when I walked into the courtyard along with twenty other missionaries, one young girl made eye contact with me, walked straight up to me and wrapped her arms around me. *She did not let go.* She must have seen my salt and pepper hair and assumed I was a mother. She had so much love for me in her eyes. *I wanted to move away, and then I heard Jesus say to me, "Let her hold you." It was sweltering hot, and we were all sweaty, but at that moment, it just did not matter. She mattered. Her needs mattered. And I surrendered.*

We were asked by Toni Hauch, who was a team leader with Father Tony, to bring something that we thought the Holy Spirit would want us to share while we were on the mission trip. I brought Charlie even though I kept hearing from the evil one, "Don't take that; it's silly to take that." I trusted, though, that it would be something special for the least of my brothers and sisters. It would end up meaning a lot to them. I also brought items from my sewing kit, all my buttons, threads, needles, and pieces of cloth, to teach the girls to sew. Twenty missionaries and I taught girls to sew that afternoon. Then I donated these supplies to this place. I had more than enough sewing supplies at home.

I was beginning to understand what giving of myself to the least of those around me meant—giving of my time, talent, and treasure.

On Monday and Tuesday of that week, we built and painted two houses with the help of five Jamaican contractors. Thank goodness they were there to help us! We certainly did not know what we were doing.

God always provides what is needed if we trust him, and if it is in accordance with his will for us.

Jamaica Mission Trip - Building House - 2009

Jamaica Mission Trip - Completed House - 2009

On the day of construction, I was stung by wasps three times because I wore bright yellow nurse's pants (team leaders advised purchasing them to stay cool)! I did not expect this to happen.

The total square footage of the houses, individually, was about 550 square feet, small in size by any US standard, but a mansion to many Jamaicans. Father Tony blessed both houses, and several small gifts were given to the new homeowners.

We also visited Ellersly Pen in Kingston, Jamaica. Some of the communities were referred to as "pens." From what I saw, these areas looked like pig pens because the conditions were so bad. This particular area we drove into, to visit the elementary school children, was surrounded by a high chain-link fence. We were told we would be there only briefly and would need to leave quickly. We went inside the school to find that the children were clean, wearing uniforms, and they sang the ABC song with us. There were many babies in cribs and no one to hold them, which saddened me greatly, but we were told that they were being cared for and loved by the staff throughout the day.

We went to the Jerusalem Children's home, one of eight Mustard Seed communities for severely mentally and physically disabled children. Within the facility was an area for HIV-positive children who were abandoned by their families. The staff informed us that before this place existed, these people were considered "throwaway children" who were caged and hosed down with water, and not fed very much. The founder of this place sought mercy for these people by establishing the Jerusalem Children's home.

Now, something I will never forget—as if the last few stories were already difficult to write—the staff led us into a room that had a young girl sitting on a chair. She appeared to be an older teenager, or a woman in her twenties. She was severely malnourished and could not control her bodily functions. She was sitting in a dark room. The room smelled of urine. I then felt moved to place my hands on her shoulders just to let her know someone was with her. Then I left the room, to let others draw near to her as well.

God used my past severe suffering to tug at my heart, to draw me closer to her in a compassionate way. This is how he works.

After I left the room, I was singled out by one of the Down Syndrome young adults. He took my hand, and with the rest of my team in tow, we all walked to the other side of the facility. He held my hand for about fifteen minutes. They told us before we came into the facility that if this happened, just to "go with it" but to watch out for each other's safety. My other team members kept an eye on me as this young man and I walked hand-in-hand through the facility. Our team leaders told us that when we are in these facilities, the residents can sometimes surprise you, and you can be at risk of getting hurt.

During this trip, there were several times that people latched on to us and were very strong and unwilling to detach themselves. Another team member named John, was my guardian angel on this trip, and helped me several times. I was so grateful he was there.

We visited a homeless shelter where I met a young man in his early twenties sitting by himself, who had happy eyes. I went over to him, introduced myself, and said, "Did you know you have happy eyes?" He said, "Yes." I asked him if he was happy. He said he was happy, but he was unemployed. As we talked, I realized that his eyes looked like the eyes of my brother, Jimmy. They were a bit darker, but I felt as though I was talking to my brother. It was the oddest thing to me.

I had read about this kind of thing happening, and heard before the trip that we might feel a connection with someone on the mission trip, as though we were talking with a family member, and would not want to leave them behind.

I told this homeless man I was not worried about him, and that I thought he would be fine. He said, "Why would you worry about me?" At that moment, I began to choke up because I could not tell him how much I wanted to take him home with me, to help him, and I did not want to leave him there as a homeless person. I then told him how much he reminded me of my younger brother, and he said, "We both believe in Christ, so we ARE brother and sister." At that very moment, I saw Jesus in his face as he was ministering to me! Out of hundreds of people I saw and dozens I spoke with on that mission trip, *he was ministering to me as though Jesus was alive.* He then said, "Do not worry about me." Well, I could not speak and was tearing up.

I asked him if I could take his picture, but he did not want me to, so I did not. Instead, I said, "I will remember you, especially when all I have to do is look at the eyes of my brother, Jimmy. Will you remember me?" He said, "I will try to." I said that Jesus is with him, and we hugged goodbye.

We were all told to go into the shelter, and as soon as I got inside the structure, I broke down in tears as I felt I was abandoning my little brother. Several women comforted me. The priest gave us another fifteen minutes to spend with the homeless. I went back outside to find the young man to provide him with a prayer card. He was gone. I continued to cry. *Father Tony took me aside to say that sometimes the poorest of the poor minister to us at the same time we are ministering to them.* When I returned home, the young man remained on my mind, and I sketched his face on a drawing pad, so I would not forget him.

We visited the Alpha Boys School. There, we were entertained by an orchestra band of boys aged 15-19 years old, and danced to their music. We also saw their woodworking and printing workshops where they learn new skills for possible future employment. The mission of this school is "the empowerment and personal transformation of young people through education and skills training."[29]

Another place we visited, Golden Age Home, is a home for some of the most severely mentally and physically disabled people in Jamaica, as well as elderly parents who have been abandoned by their family members. Several elderly ladies sang for us. They loved that we listened to them.

Soon after we arrived, a mentally challenged older man singled me out of the group, wrapped both of his arms around me, and planted a huge kiss on my cheek. He was physically very strong. He asked me if I was married, and I said, "At one time." He asked if I was married now, and I said, "no." *He said we would get married Sunday!* Later he brought me a one-inch square piece of paper and put it in the palm of my hand and said we would get married Sunday. I said, "No, I don't think so."

Then I walked Charlie, the marionette, over to one of the other older men with Alzheimer's disease who was sitting with Toni (team leader) on a bench. I rested Charlie's head on his knee, and he then got a huge smile on his face, giggled, and petted Charlie. It was a tender moment to witness this interaction.

Some with Alzheimer's disease believed he was a real dog. He has bright blue fur and very long legs. Another elderly person, a woman, was ecstatic to see Charlie!

---

[29] To learn more, visit www.alphaboysschool.org.

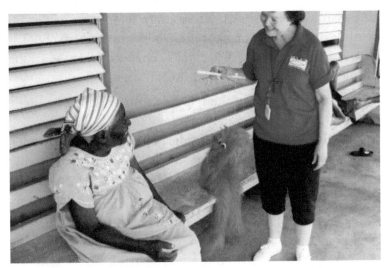

Jamaica Mission Trip - Sharing Charlie (the marionette) – 2009
(Picture taken by Toni Hauch)

A little schoolboy came to see his mother, who was a staff employee there, and he saw Charlie. Then the first older man who said we would marry me came over to me again, pulled the boy over to him, stood in front of me, and asked if I could cook. I said, "Yes." He then pointed to the mountains and said, "house." *At that moment, I realized that he was assembling his family, and I was to be his wife, and the boy and I would be his family.* Once again, my fellow missionary guardian angel, John, who saw what was happening, came over to rescue me. We decided it was time to leave, not knowing what might happen next.

Again, God was leading me down a particular path, one step at a time, to show me what he had in store for me. We cannot possibly know all that God wants us to know all-at-once. "For my thoughts are not your thoughts, neither are your ways my ways, says the Lord." (Is. 55:8)

All the steps of this journey took place at specific times, and when God decided it was the right time for these particular steps to happen. None of this was ever planned by me. I would not have known what to plan because I had no idea of where I was going or what I would do. Jokingly, my dad would have been shocked at this journey of mine, simply because I did not have a plan!

A common saying in Christian circles is, "If you want to make God laugh, tell him your plans."

Something profound I learned from the missionary work in Jamaica was that many of us in the United States have it backwards. US citizens in general are financially prosperous and not necessarily spiritually wealthy; whereas, the poor people of Jamaica are spiritually wealthy and not financially wealthy. Who is better off? In observing the poor, even in their physical misery, I saw they were joyful in their faith in God and Jesus Christ. *And I knew from my own empty lifestyle in the United States, after having climbed the ladder of financial success, that my life was spiritually empty in comparison to theirs.*

During the trip, the team leaders gave us something to inspire us spiritually every day. The following is from Father Tony of our team. It was titled "Thoughts to Ponder."

If you woke up this morning with more health than illness, you are more blessed than the 1 million who will not survive this week.

If you have never experienced the danger of battle, the loneliness of imprisonment, the agony of torture, or the pangs of starvation, you are ahead of 1 billion people in the world.

If you can attend a church without fear of harassment, arrest, torture, or death, you are more blessed than 3 billion people in this world.

If you have food in the refrigerator, clothes on your back, a roof over your head, and a safe place to sleep, you are richer than 75% of the world.

If you have money in the bank, in your wallet, in your purse, and spare change in a dish somewhere in your home, you are among the top 8% of the world's most wealthy.

If you could have read this message, you would be more blessed than 2 billion people in the world who cannot read.

My prayer for all of us is that we develop a sense of gratitude and give thanks and praise to God every day for all the blessings we have, by virtue of the fact we live in the United States, instead of complaining about what we do not have. We express gratitude by our kindness to one another, and our generosity to 75% of the world who live in conditions that we cannot even imagine.[30]

I, of course, was fulfilled with the love of my sons and their families, but I began to see there was so much more one could have in life; that is, a personal relationship with Jesus, and giving of oneself to others. My sons were grown by this time, and I was an empty-nester, so it made sense to me that God would show me this through a missionary trip to Jamaica. It was time.

This trip happened one year before my calling to become a Catholic sister, and after I had heard the voice of Jesus for one year.[31] The following thoughts are the reflections I had after I left Jamaica.

Being a missionary made me realize that to become more holy, we have to achieve our true purpose in life, which is to serve others, especially those who are the least of our brothers and sisters. This is what provides balance in the world between the materially rich and the suffering poor, and also between the spiritually rich and spiritually poor.

---

[30] Based on Donella H. Meadows, "State of the Village Report," *The Global Citizen* syndicated column (May 31, 1990), The Sustainability Institute, MA.
[31] 2008 – Welcomed Jesus Christ into my heart. 2009 – Unplanned mission trip. 2010 – Unexpected calling from Jesus.

God's Providence can occur between the rich and the poor. We trust that God will provide. Every time I give of my wealth, as little as it might be today as a retiree, God seems to repay me with more, proportionately, than what I gave. *I see this because my eyes are open now.*

The missionary experience prepared me for the next step to follow the calling from Jesus. Yet, I did not know at the time what the next step would be. Looking back, I can see this mission trip helped to prepare me to become a sister. Just after the trip, I created a new little prayer with Jesus' help during my silent time with him:

Jesus says to me today,
You are walking in my footsteps.
You are worthy to do so.
No more tears, no more tears.
You are filled with the Holy Spirit.
You are filled with joy now.
Be happy.

I realized that I was beginning to follow the ways of Jesus as I worked face-to-face with many disadvantaged people. Although I had confessed my sins and was absolved by a priest, I continued to hurt and cry during my life after divorce, especially during Mass. God wanted me to minister to the disadvantaged. He had to show this to me before I could become a sister. Then our missionary priest, Father Tony, wisely advised me to "let go and let God."

My heart and soul were being mended.

Up to this point, I knew I was beginning to change, one step at a time, and by God's design for me. I did not know his plan. No clue. Where I was going and what I would be doing, I did not know. I also did not know exactly how my life was about to change.

Specific things were being told to me by this very positive voice, not only in my personal life but also at work. I listened. I discerned. I prayed. I was finally open to hearing what Jesus told me to do.

Everything at work became effortless. I had no worries or concerns because I knew the things Jesus was telling me were correct and good. And I knew God was in charge, not me. I no longer held on so tightly to my areas of responsibility; instead, I released them to others, providing the necessary training, while giving others the opportunity to grow to a higher level of responsibility in the workplace as well. I suddenly had trust in God and Jesus as I never had before.

One year later, I heard Jesus calling me to become a nun.

As background, nearly a decade prior, my father had passed away, leaving our mother a widow. She eventually moved into the home of my sister, Dot, to live with her and her husband, Mike. Remember our large family? We would take turns spending time with Mom on the weekends at their house, taking her to the beautician to have her hair done and to have lunch.

On August 6, 2010, I was with my Mom at their house when I received the calling from Jesus. She was right there with me on this important day. I cannot think of a better form of support than having my Mom right by my side that morning, because I did not have a clue of what was about to happen.

At 7:30 a.m. Jesus flooded me with "stuff." It is a phenomenon I had never experienced before. I refer to it as a flood because it seemed as though many things were flowing through me all at once. And I call it stuff because what I received was a variety of many, many things I was told to do, all good things, and all in the same moment. I was overwhelmed during this moment, trying to process as much as I could with my little human brain.

To be clear, and as I stated in the beginning of this book, these were examples of divine promptings that were only meant for me, not to become messages for the whole world. Everything the Holy Spirit, Jesus, God, or Mary told me, has been only meant for me, no one else. This is important to share as I would not want anyone to think, that I believe I am a prophet. I am not, and do not aspire to be, a prophet. As Christians, we are encouraged to develop a personal relationship with God, and in doing so, we can develop a level of communication, talking to him and actively listening to him. These conversations are nurtured over time.

Returning to the story of the calling, I had no idea of what was happening. At first, I just listened. It was so much information. Thousands of bits of information were coming at me all at the same time. I sat on the side of Mom's bed, being still and quiet so I could hear and receive what Jesus was giving me. I was not aware of what Mom was doing except that she was awake and still in bed. She must have been still and quiet too, as I did not hear her.

It was the voice of Jesus again. I heard his voice for two years after I welcomed him into my heart with great yearning. There was no other explanation for what I was about to hear. I was not on any new medicine. I even had a Top-Secret security clearance that was reviewed and updated every five years by an agency investigator who conducted an extensive interview with me, due to the job I held. What was happening?

I could only process in my mind the first four things Jesus told me. They were enough to digest by themselves, without all the other information that followed these first four things I heard.

➤ Jesus told me to become a nun.

> ➢ He told me that every day I am not serving the suffering, I am making them wait for me.

> ➢ He told me to write the book.

> ➢ He told me to quit watching so much TV, so I can get all this done.

These things were completely unprecedented. Prior to hearing the voice of Jesus during the previous two years, I was a negative person with a temper. I am Irish. My maiden name is McDonald for Pete's sake! We have tempers. To hear such good and positive things during those two years, was curious. And now that I knew his voice, he ordered me to do particular things—these four things—and so much more I could not process fast enough. It was impossible to process the rest of what he gave me, so I let go of it.

Once the flood of information stopped, I began to cry uncontrollably because it was overwhelming to receive these things, especially these particular things. I have no reason to doubt that it was the powerful voice of the Son of God himself. It was more than I could handle at that moment.

My Mom asked me why I was crying, and I could not say, because I did not know how to express what I had just experienced. Then she cried. We cried together, and she still did not have any idea why I was crying this much so early in the morning. She also was not used to seeing me cry because I did not cry very often anyway. All I could tell her was that Jesus flooded me with stuff. She consoled me in a compassionate way, as mothers often do.

It was at this time that I also received the answer of who I would spend the rest of my life with, not with one man, a human being on this earth, but with Jesus Christ as my best friend. Since 2010, the year of my calling, I have been content in my chastity and no longer yearn to be with someone. My joys in life are continuing to be a mother and grandmother, and helping those who are in anguish.

Spending time with my family brings me great joy in the few times we can align our schedules to do so. They are the most precious moments for me. There is never enough time to spend with those we love. I pray every single day that we will all be together in heaven someday, asking for Saint Monica's intercession, and offering my Communion for them at every Mass.

Since that first flood of information from Jesus, this phenomenon still happens to me about three times a year, and they are always profound events. I cherish these times. I try to document everything he tells me.

The first order from him, to become a nun, was enough by itself. For two weeks, I walked around in a daze, not believing what Jesus told me to do. I told him, "You MUST have the wrong woman, Lord. Me? You can't be serious! What?" I was a great sinner. How could he possibly want me to be a nun? How could this even be possible as I was fifty-five years old when he called me (besides the brief tap on the shoulder when I was fourteen). I did not know at the time that there were organizations of Catholic sisters who would consider accepting older women – another discovery! This was another part of the journey I will share later in this book.

For two weeks, I did not share this calling with anyone except my mother, while I tried to understand what was happening to me. I was not a young woman and did not fit the qualifying criteria of women entering a religious order, so how could it be that Jesus was telling me to become a nun? I was working in a high-paid government job with great responsibility at the time. I was a divorced Mom with three grown sons and a grandchild, at this time. *None of this made sense except that I knew his voice, so how could I say "no" to Jesus, to God?* That was *not* an option, is what I thought.

I was not worthy. Or was I?

If God's path for me was to truly become a nun, I cannot believe he would have that much faith in me and love me enough to have the honor to serve as a nun. I would never have believed that I was worthy of such a sacred life. He had faith in me and trusted that I could do this, more than I ever would have imagined. I would never have thought I was worthy because of my past sins.

I now understand the full circle, that if I was a great sinner, and I am wholeheartedly sorry for my sins, and ask forgiveness, he forgives me, and I begin again, renewed in his Holy Spirit. In that transformation, a person is reborn, to become virtually a new person, and that change allows us to go on to do great things for him. *I would learn later that he expects great things of us. "For much that is given, much is expected" (Lk. 12:48).*

I was beginning to learn that God will always have more confidence in me than I will ever have in myself. I have to believe that what he calls me to do, *is what I can do, with his grace.* Discerning what he is calling us to do, though, takes time and prayer, and I will discuss this in a later chapter.

Another good friend of mine, Marsha, once said to me, "He doesn't want the saints. He wants the aints!" This makes sense. Who better to bring to those who need help to become better versions of themselves, than those who learned how? Becoming more holy takes work, and sharing the steps of that work is what he expects of me now.

Later I learned we do not always go in a straight line on our faith journeys, that sometimes he takes us on detours. And many times, we do not know why, until later. For example,

Jesus called me to be a nun. In the Code of Canon Law,[32] we learn that a nun is cloistered and does not normally leave cloistered life; however, if she leaves cloistered life, she then becomes a sister.

Later in this book, I will discuss how I ultimately joined an association of the faithful, rather than a traditional order. Both fall under the Code of Canon Law, but they are in different categories. Although Jesus told me to be a nun, I am a sister, and I trust he is completely okay with this, considering the good fruits of the Holy Spirit[33] that result from prison ministry, and other ministries of mercy. And this work is consistent with his request of us to visit those in prison (Mt. 25:35-45), the suffering imprisoned Christ.

"It is a paradox that you cannot have faith until you make the leap of faith, and you cannot have trust until you decide to trust. So how do we begin? We start by praying, 'I believe; help my unbelief!' (Mk. 9:24). Eventually, however, we must set aside our doubts, accept God at his word, and 'just do it.'"[34]

The only way I could go forward, since I recognized him as Jesus, and as the source of the command to me to become a nun, was to trust him, and let him lead me. Such an arrogant thought, to *let* him lead me!

The second command was easy to understand – Every day I am not serving the suffering, I am making them wait for me. I had never served the least of my brothers and sisters.

---

[32] To learn more, go to www.vatican.va/archive/cod-iuris-canonici/cic_index_en.html. Additionally, a simple summary of the differences between nuns and sisters is: *www.canonlawmadeeasy.com/2009/03/19/whats-the-difference-between-sisters-and-nuns*.

[33] "But the fruit of the Holy Spirit is love, joy, peace, patience, kindness, goodness, faithfulness, gentleness, self-control; against such there is no law" (Gal. 5:22-23).

[34] Woodene Koenig-Bricker, *Abundance through Stewardship* (Huntington, Indiana: *Our Sunday Visitor*, 2004).

I did not have a history of social work at all before I was a sister. The way he expressed it to me was surprising, that every day I am not serving the suffering, I am making them wait. They are waiting for me. He made it personal.

I was dragging my feet, being self-serving, being comfortable in my life. It was time to give back. It was time for God's Providence to kick in. *God expects me to give of my time, talent, and treasure.*

The third command, to write the book, has taken a long time to start. I collected significant writings that made a spiritual impression on me. I documented unexplained mystical events for the day when I might write the book. Jesus did not tell me again to write the book after the calling in 2010, until January 2018. As he had done before, he flooded me with stuff all-at-once, and one of these things was telling me again to write the book.

I still did not feel motivated, until the "Last Drop" event that happened in the summer of 2019, which I shared in the preface of this book. This three-day event motivated me because the thought of *not* having *any* priests in the entire world to celebrate Mass was frightening.

Our priests are the current authority of Jesus Christ. Without priests, we cannot receive his Precious Body and Precious Blood. They serve *in persona Christi*, which is "in the person of Christ" in Latin.

Jesus gave me the focus of this book as an invitation to the reader to consider religious life through the journey of what can happen when one middle-aged woman says "yes" to the calling. This spiritual autobiography is about one journey. A person's journey is unique to them, yet it can be similar in comparison to other journeys.

He also provided me with the Table of Contents and told me to prepare a space to work. He was leading me through the steps of writing a book with his divine inspiration. Then a fellow prison ministry team member, Judy, asked her friend if she could help to guide me through the steps of writing this book, because I had never written a book. Her friend, Lyn, has been a tremendous help to me because she has a history of working in publishing. She is also an excellent source of encouragement. *And she told me that she happened to have been praying for something to do! This was God's arrangement for both of us.*

The last order Jesus gave me on the day of my calling, to quit watching so much TV so I can get all this done, was such a shock. This was how I relaxed after a long day of work and did not see too much wrong with this at the time. Why would I tell myself to quit watching so much TV? If I enjoyed watching TV, for what reason would I stop?

Jesus was the only one who knew just how much television I was watching. There would have been no logical reason to tell myself to stop watching so much TV after work. Eventually, I watched far less television though. He was right. He knew, and I knew, that to make changes in my life, I had to sacrifice watching so much television after work and on the weekends.

With time, prayer, meditation, discernment, and sharing with other Catholics, I began to accept this calling, to surrender my life to God, and to serve others. *I remain a mother and grandmother, of course. These bonds can never be broken.*

More curious things began to happen. Soon my agency would *suddenly* offer early retirements to employees who met specific eligibility requirements, and offered bonuses as an incentive to retire. Much to my surprise, I met the criteria to retire early from the federal government. Discerning this decision to follow the calling became easier, with an incentive to retire! And it was very curious how this was offered at the exact time I was considering retiring early. God works in mysterious ways, doesn't he? This was not a coincidence.

I spent much more time in prayer, at Mass, retreats, reading Catholic resources, and meeting with my priest, Father Brian. He was the first person I met with after the calling, other than talking about this with my mother.

Eventually, I told my sons, ex-husband, siblings, parents, and my supervisor what was happening to me, and that I would retire early from the government to follow this calling, giving up one-third of my pension. Everyone was shocked, as I was, and probably thought I had lost my mind. But I knew I had not. I knew this was of the spiritual realm, something new and different, a new life, seeing things in new ways, following the ways of Jesus Christ.

My oldest son, Chris, expressed that "If she is happy, I am happy." Even though no one fully understood what was happening to me, including myself, I was moving in a positive [and joyful] direction in my life.

As I write this book ten years after the calling, I can say that my family and friends now know I am serious about my new life, and this is not a fleeting desire, or something else. The longer I minister, the more understanding and accepting some family members have become.

If I were in their shoes, I would have indeed wondered why in the world she was making such a drastic change in life. There is too much to share about this journey in a phone call or a short visit, although I wanted to share it all with them. Now, I am grateful Jesus told me to write the book, to be able to share this journey.

After the calling, I began reading *The Life of D. L. Moody, Passion for Souls.*[35] Someone must have recommended this to me. I learned that God is not only calling me to become a nun, but that he is also asking me to help him bring souls to Christ. I never would have thought that I would have ever been a person that could help even one person come to the cross, let alone bring myself to the cross. *God has a way of strengthening our faith in his own mysterious ways, and in ways we sometimes view to be illogical and unreasonable.* We learn that with him, all things are possible, and this is our faith. "With God, all things are possible" (Mt. 19:26).

Author D.L. Moody said, "If God calls a man to a work, he will be with him in that work, and he will succeed no matter what the obstacles may be."

This means I have to trust God that he will give me the grace I need to do whatever he asks me to do. He opens doors that otherwise would be closed. He even opens doors at times when we are not ready. It is like jumping on a fast train and holding on for dear life! And as long as I can hop on that fast train, after discerning what he asks of me, I will do what he asks, because I trust him. Sounds unreasonable and illogical, doesn't it? We think with human minds, not like God. **Yet we find freedom as we change how we think, while allowing God to change us, following his [what we might view to be] illogical ways.**

Then I learned that according to scripture, "My brothers, the case may arise among you of someone straying from the truth, and of another bringing him back. Remember this: the person who brings a sinner back from his way will save his soul from death and cancel a multitude of sins" (Jm. 5:19-20).

---

[35] D.L. Moody, *The Life of D. L. Moody, Passion for Souls* (Chicago: Moody Publishers, 1997), 6.

When I realized what Jesus was calling me to do, to help others find their way to the cross, to serve those who suffer, the thought of bringing even one person back was humbling to me. *That God would trust me to do this with HIS people is overwhelming to me.* Since that time, he has placed many people on my path who are seeking answers and consolation. I am grateful he called me in these last years of my life.

I visited two of my sons, their families, and my brother shortly after the calling. I was not retired yet, and I missed my family. Now that I had a calling to become a nun, I knew that if I was accepted into an order, I would be in formation and living away from my family once again. I wrestled with this, not knowing what the future would hold if I continued to follow the calling from Jesus. What if I did not make it through formation? Then what?

I was excited about this new journey because it felt good, and it felt right. My sons and their families were self-sufficient and focused on building their lives together. Whenever we need support, we try to help each other, as families do. We love each other.

I understand the unconditional love of God now, and I want everyone to know about this. This can take time to learn as everyone is at a different level of spirituality.

I also want those who suffer to know that they can hold on to hope every day, even if there does not seem to be any sign of hope. They have the hope of heaven and the hope of knowing Christ at a deeper level. I want them to know that when they suffer, they are not alone.

After the calling and before I retired, I saw the San Damiano Cross in church and at a retreat center, but I did not know its history. It drew me in, in a mysterious way that I could not explain. A priest explained that it has a history of drawing people whose hearts are open, one of which was Saint Francis of Assisi.

San Damiano Cross - 2010

Saint Francis was gazing upon this cross at a time when God told him to "Rebuild my church." He thought this meant he was supposed to rebuild the physically-battered church, which he did physically with his followers, but God *also* meant to rebuild his Church with believers. Saint Francis began to evangelize. I believe God was telling me the same thing when he drew me to this cross, to help him to rebuild his Church, one person at a time. And this is what I do every day when I meet people in public, in church, and in ministries. I am grateful to have this opportunity.

Saint Ignatius of Loyola, founder of the Society of Jesus, wrote, "...you are his soldiers with a special rank and a special pay...to work for his honor and service. His pay is the incalculable gifts of his glory that he has prepared for you and promised you, without his gaining anything. And if these payments were not enough, he has made himself our pay, giving himself to us as our brother in our flesh, on the cross as the price of our salvation, in the Eucharist as our sustainer and companion for our pilgrimage. What a miserable soldier a man would be if all these payments were not enough to make him work for the honor of such a Prince!"[36] Saint Ignatius is clear about the "pay" of those who serve the suffering Christ. *We are not to expect anything in return for our services to others.*

Author Matthew Kelly helps us to understand how to become the best version of ourselves. He asks, "What is holiness? Holiness is all the incredible things God will do in you and through you if you make yourself available to him."[37] Isn't this what Our Blessed Mother Mary did when the Angel Gabriel announced to her that she would give birth to the Messiah? It was her fiat, her "yes," her faith we hope to imitate when God calls us to serve.

And "Thus [apostle] Paul can say, "It is no longer I who live, but Christ who lives in me" (Gal. 2:20).

The father of the prodigal son said, "This son of mine was lost and has been found; he was dead and has come back to life" (Lk. 15:11-32).

All of these references are about listening for the will of God for us, being open to change, discerning through prayer about change, and making changes *if the changes are in accordance with God's will for us.* Discerning takes time. It is not something that should be rushed.

We must look for the good fruit of the Holy Spirit of God when we discern his will for us. And this also takes time in ardent prayerful discernment.

---

[36] Ignatius of Loyola, *Personal Writings*, trans. Joseph A. Munitiz (London: Penguin, 1997), 175.
[37] Matthew Kelly, *Rediscover Catholicism*, 2nd ed. (Erlanger, Kentucky: The Dynamic Catholic Institute, 2010), 74.

Finally, I close this chapter with a quote based on writings taken from an Advent booklet, "My journey doesn't end when I 'find Christ.' Finding Christ sets me on the way, but the road is often a difficult one. When I find Christ, I am no longer adrift, but there are still many miles at sea to go, with storms, fog, and darkness."[38]

I could not have said it better. My journey will continue until I pass on to purgatory, then to heaven, hopeful this will be my end.

Questions for the reader to contemplate: Will I spend time in the silence, in prayer, to discern God's will for me? Is it possible I might have what God needs right now, my specific time, talent, and treasure, to serve the least of our brothers and sisters? Has he already tapped me on the shoulder, but I do not know where to start?

---

[38] *Little Books of the Diocese of Saginaw, Inc: Advent/Christmas Season: Little Blue Book* 2019, based on the writings of Bishop Ken Untener (Saginaw, Diocese of Saginaw Inc., 2019).

CHAPTER 4
SPIRITUAL WARFARE AND PRAYER

-◢◤-

Do you believe that Satan exists in this earthly life? If the answer is yes, do you think God exists as well? If there is evil, there is good; therefore, God exists. The devil's greatest success is the denial of God's existence.

Many people today do not want to think about the forces of good and evil, because it is either too overwhelming to contemplate, or they are afraid of what they might learn or experience.

If we pay attention to how the spiritual realm works, we then understand better what is happening in our own individual lives. Ignoring the spiritual side of ourselves is dangerous. Why? Because if we are not fully aware, we can become victims of evil, without even knowing it is taking place.

The evil one is just as present in our environment as God is in our lives. He waits, just as God does, for us to turn to him. We choose to do evil acts, or we can choose to turn our backs on the temptations of evil. It is a choice. Evil offends God. As Christians, we choose to please God, or we choose to entertain the evil one.

As we mature into adulthood, we can also become more mature in our faith, dedicated, loyal, and responsible, giving all glory and praise to God for all things, and serving those who suffer.

Knowledge is power. Knowledge is practical. Knowledge is necessary to survive. We have heard these words before, normally heard in the workplace. They apply to our spiritual growth as well. Human beings have mental, physical, emotional, and spiritual components. Each of these deserve attention to maintain overall wellness.

Preparing ourselves and our children in the Christian faith is essential for those times in life that are most difficult, and for when unexplained phenomenon happens to us. We also need to know the dangers that exist, to understand how to avoid sin, and to teach our children right from wrong, so they will learn how to protect themselves against evil, especially as they grow older. They may become vulnerable and fall victim to evil and the loss of heaven, unless they have been given a strong foundation in the faith.

There are constant threats in our world today, including threats of being drawn into evil practices. In some cases, a person might not realize this is happening before it is too late.

After I received the calling from Jesus, there was darkness around me for about a month that I could not explain. I had never experienced something like this before. Instinctively, I knew I needed to talk with a priest about this. I met with Father Brian, who told me this was normal and expected after receiving a calling to become a nun. He said it is probably the evil one trying to scare me away from my calling.

Father informed me that I would need to file for an annulment of my marriage to have a clear path to the cross. At the time of my calling, I had a civil divorce and no annulment. I applied to the diocese Tribunal for consideration. The answer came while I was in formation. I will share the details of this in a later chapter.

I was grateful to have access to a Catholic priest who could put in perspective for me what this dark cloud was about. He gave me a blessing and soon the dark cloud went away. No medicine or medical treatment was necessary. I did not have depression or anxiety, except for a healthy, reasonable fear of the unknown. I was about to experience the adventure of the calling itself, a new beginning, something I was unfamiliar with.

While on this journey, I learned a great deal about what spiritual warfare is and how it works, although one can never know enough about this subject.

Spiritual warfare is the battle that takes place for our souls on a daily basis. *Our choice is whether we will please God, or entertain the evil one.* God gave us our earthly life and promises eternal life with him in heaven. Satan began his existence with God, fell from grace with God, and now works to steal souls from God through sin.

The warfare can be within ourselves, in our own minds. It can also be between two or more people at a time. Resolving conflict quickly and efficiently is most desirable so that we can return to a place of inner peace and maintain harmony with others. Sometimes this is not possible at the time of the conflict, but may become possible at a later point in time.

When we sin, we willingly distance ourselves from God. Many types of sin offend God. It is a choice. Like criminal actions, sinful actions come with consequences. Tobit tells us in the Bible that, "If you turn to him with all your heart and with all your soul, to do what is true before him, then he will turn to you and will not hide his face from you" (Tob. 13:6).

We turn our backs on God when we sin. Yet when we are remorseful of our sins, seeking mercy and forgiveness, he is right there waiting for us to turn to him, to forgive us, as we see in this scripture:

Isaiah 1:16-18

Wash yourselves clean!
Put away your misdeeds from before my eyes;
Cease doing evil; learn to do good.
Make justice your aim; redress the wronged,
Hear the orphan's plea, defend the widow.
Come now, let us set things right,
Says the Lord:
Though your sins be like scarlet,
They may become white as snow;
Though they be crimson red,
They may become white as wool.

There is hope for everyone to become a better version of themselves, for their sins to be wiped away through confession with a priest, to start over. And through this process, we become stronger and more convicted in our faith when we commit *not* to sin again. My strategy is to decide *not* to commit the same sins over and over again.

We have a choice. Choose *not* to sin in the first place. Choose good, not evil.

Some Catholics think it is okay to commit a sin, confess it to a priest, receive absolution, then commit the sin again, with no interest or effort to truly change who they are, in order to become more holy. This is not the right way to practice our faith as Catholics. It is not okay. We are not fooling anyone except ourselves anyway when we do this, because God sees everything we do.

One of the first things to know about spiritual warfare is to understand our enemy, as discussed in Doctor Paul

Thigpen's book, *Manual for Spiritual Warfare.*[39] This resource is easy to understand and practical.

Satan is crafty. He knows our weaknesses and temptations. He will pursue us relentlessly to tempt us to sin. It can be a constant battle with him. It takes work and daily perseverance to overcome his temptations.

When you are tempted or attacked by the evil one, the quickest and most successful way I know of to get rid of him is to simply say, "Jesus, Mary, and Joseph, help me!"

When we deviate from the teachings of Jesus, we deviate from God.

No one is exempt from sin. Sin happens to the wealthy, the poor, the healthy, the sick, priests, deacons, religious sisters and brothers, lay people—literally everyone.

We were given the Ten Commandments of God, and we were given the teachings, values, and virtues of Jesus Christ in the New Testament. We are taught right from wrong through this guidance. His teachings are timeless and good.

Our formation directress in Tijuana, Mexico, Madrè Anna Maria, told me once, "Diablo is very angry with you."[40] At that time, I did not even know who "diablo" was. She was helping me to understand this part of my journey, to expect that I would be attacked because of my "yes" to Jesus to become a nun. I was to become his hands and feet on this earth. The evil one did not want me to be successful, working as a vessel for Jesus. This would mean bringing more souls to Christ, and Satan does not want that.

---

[39] Paul Thigpen, *Manual for Spiritual Warfare* (Charlotte, North Carolina: Tan Books, 2015).
[40] Diablo is Spanish for devil.

What is important is not to be afraid. Throughout the Bible, we read, "Be not afraid" (1 Thess. 5:17).[41] The evil one has power over us when we are afraid, and the way to overcome fear is to pray, and to pray unceasingly.

There are many things we can do to armor ourselves against evil. "Stay prayed up" as we say in Christian circles. Receive the Eucharist at Catholic Mass. Pray and meditate on the rosary daily. Go to Eucharistic Adoration and spend time with the Lord. There are many more ways to wage battle against Satan and his evil spirits.

If you are attacked by Satan or other evil spirits in a significant way, seek a special blessing from a priest or deacon. Talk with other spiritually-grounded Christians you trust and share your experiences with them. Pray the Rosary together. Bless yourself with holy water that has been blessed by an ordained minister. Use blessed salt and oil for your home and other areas.

What is most important though, is building your faith foundation through constant prayer with God.

Along the way, *I also received good confirmations from God* that I was on the right track. I was beginning to see these kinds of things because my eyes were open, spiritually. I was evolving into a more mature level of faith with a better understanding of how good and evil forces work. The confirmations from God are essential on this journey, because often doubt can set in, tempting us to stop the work we are called to do.

Just as Satan tries to get in our way, God is also right there, showing us his presence every day, sometimes in the smallest ways.

---

[41] Several scriptural references are: Mt. 17:7, Mk. 5:36, and Mt. 28:10. There are many other scriptures about fear.

We cannot let Satan and his evil forces win. If we have been asked to work as the hands and feet of Jesus, then that is what we must do, and not let him talk us out of it! We must stay focused on Jesus and what he needs us to do.

One of the most beautiful, unexpected, convicting confirmations I received from God was on Christmas Eve of 2010, four months after I received the calling from Jesus. I was at the Christ the King Cathedral in Atlanta again, this time for Midnight Mass. The archbishop was the celebrant. Two of my good friends, Jen and Lop, attended with me.

From the beginning of Mass, I witnessed something unexpected and unexplainable; that is, that Jesus moved on the cross. As Mass began, I was gazing at the crucifix as I had been

Crucifix of Christ the King Cathedral, Atlanta GA - 2010

doing in recent months at other churches. I was praying, and I began to see him move on the cross. I thought I was seeing things, but later my friends said they saw him move as well. This was very reassuring to me to know that I was not the only one who saw this.

I was so excited by what I saw that I wanted to jump up and yell out to the entire congregation, "Do you see this? Do you see him moving on the cross?" Of course, I did not do this. First, I saw his jaw moving up and down and slightly turning his head as though he was speaking to the entire congregation. He was not looking at me specifically; he was talking to everyone. I could not hear what he said. I saw the biceps of his arms moving. And finally, it appeared that his torso was moving as though he was breathing. *Then I realized that he was trying to come down from the cross, but could not, as he was nailed to the cross.*

This was another significant event on my journey. I believed Jesus had a message for me that night, so I could not take my eyes off him throughout the entire Mass. This was so overwhelming to me that at one point, I felt as though I was going to faint. Jen, a doctor, applied pressure to below my nose and in between my eyes with her thumb. These were pressure points to bring blood to my head. I was overcome with lightheadedness and could not remain in the pew.

Jen was concerned I would faint after I left the pew, but I said I would be fine and just needed to get some fresh air. Just before the distribution of the Eucharist to the parishioners, I walked to the back of the church and told the usher I thought I was going to faint. He took me outside. After I came back into the church, I stayed there until it was time to receive Communion.

After Mass, the archbishop smiled at me in the midst of thirty people milling around in the narthex area of the church, as though he knew of this special message from Jesus to me. I wondered if he knew.

Later I happened to share this experience with the archbishop himself and his reaction was, "Isn't it wonderful to receive such a special gift from God, just for you?" Yes, it was wonderful, something from God himself, through his beloved son, Jesus, hanging on the cross. This was a confirmation for me to keep following the calling, knowing that suffering people are still waiting for me to help them.

The next morning, Christmas morning, I was flooded with "stuff" from Jesus again, just like it happened on the day of my calling. Again, it was too much to process because it happened in a fleeting moment. What I captured, though, was that *Jesus told me that I have to be his hands and feet because he cannot come down off the cross.* He was talking about moving on the crucifix from the night before, and telling me what it meant.

This was an overwhelming thought again, that he, Our Lord, has confidence in me to serve his suffering people on his behalf.

How would I help everyone in need, those who were still waiting for me? I experienced over time that God tends to place me with only one person at a time, to listen to. No scheduled meeting either. He provides the perfect meeting, whether it is a grocery store, the doctor's office, prison, or church; they are spontaneous meetings, arranged entirely by him.

I shared everything about this experience with Jen the next morning, on Christmas Day. She and her boyfriend said they saw Jesus move on the cross as well. I was relieved to know I wasn't the only one who saw this.

Later I learned through research of unexplained mystical phenomenon that there has been a history of these kinds of events happening through the centuries, especially at midnight Mass on Christmas Eve. Christmas Eve is an extraordinary time of the year as Christians anticipate and celebrate the arrival of the Child Jesus, whom we believe is the long-awaited Messiah. A baby.

I shared this experience with other spiritually-grounded people, including several nuns I met, who said that I definitely have a calling to become a nun. This was another confirmation that I was on the right path.

Sometimes I doubted the calling, then confirmations from God kept me focused. Do you see how Satan wants us to doubt ourselves? As I go along on my journey, I have come to know that God has got this, even though the evil one has tried many ways to keep me from my calling, from doing the work I have been called to do.

I stay close to my best friend, Jesus Christ, in constant communication with him through prayer. I trust that good always wins over evil in the end.

Father Gabriele Amorth was the Chief Exorcist of the Vatican, and performed over 70,000 exorcisms in a thirty-year time frame. He died in 2016 and is known as the world's most famous exorcist. He fought in WWII and went to law school before being accepted into seminary to become a Catholic Priest. Then God called him to fight demonic influence. His book is another resource for a deeper level of understanding of the forces of good and evil.[42]

Here are my thoughts about the existence of God and Satan. If there is no Satan, no evil in this world, no temptations to be concerned about, how could there be a need for exorcisms? Research documented accounts of demonic possession and discern this. Additionally, researching documented accounts of Eucharistic miracles, and healings at Marian apparition sites, lend credence to the Catholic faith and belief in God. I also believe these are the types of evidence that seekers must carefully study in order to answer the question of whether God exists.

And there are always good blessings that come from things we perceive to be bad. Sometimes the blessings are referred to as the silver lining. Sometimes people blame God for the bad things that happen to them or family members. God allows these bad things to happen for a reason, and we

---

[42] Father Gabriele Amorth with Elisabetta Fezzi, *Father Amorth: My Battle Against Satan* (Manchester, New Hampshire: Sophia Institute Press, 2018).

may never know what that reason is while we are on this earth, but certainly when we arrive in heaven, we will know all things.

His ways are not our ways (Is. 55:8).

Accepting God's will for us in all things, surrendering what we cannot handle, back to him, is the way to inner peace. *My journey has included many unexplainable things, that are illogical and unreasonable in our way of thinking.* Many of these things have been part of the way to my inner peace.

I *let* God be in control. This is such an arrogant statement for me to say, but in our spiritual maturation, this is exactly what we are doing; that is, finally letting him be in control.

During a retreat weekend, we were given the following guide (author unknown). It is simple to follow, easy to understand, and a true reflection of how a person changes as they find inner peace.

Guide to Inner Peace

A tendency to think and act spontaneously rather than from fears based on past experience.
An unmistakable ability to enjoy each moment.
A loss of interest in judging others.
A loss of interest in judging self.
A loss of interest in conflict.
A loss of interest in interpreting the actions of others.
A loss of ability to worry.
Frequent overwhelming episodes of appreciation.
Contented feelings of connectedness with others and with nature.
Frequent attacks of smiling through the heart.
Increasing susceptibility to love extended by others, as well as the uncontrollable urge to extend it.

An increasing ability to let things happen rather than to manipulate them and make them happen.

On April 21, 2011, Holy Thursday of the Easter Triduum,[43] I was traveling home from my agency headquarters in Washington, D.C., and unexpectedly saw a sign that I recognized. It was the sign for the National Shrine of the Immaculate Conception. I did not plan to visit this place even though I had been there before and loved this place of peace.

If you have never experienced the beauty of the journey through the Easter Triduum of Holy Thursday, Good Friday, and Holy Saturday, please give yourself this gift. Easter Sunday is at the end of the Triduum journey.

While I was waiting for Mass to start at the shrine on Holy Thursday, I felt a strong urge to speak with a nun. I thought surely there would be a nun at this shrine. I asked the lady at the welcome desk if she knew of a nun I could talk to. She said she did. *I became very anxious because I did not even have any questions for her and did not know what to say. I just knew I was supposed to speak with a nun!*

A young sister in full habit and veil presented herself to me after a few minutes of waiting. I asked if she had some time to speak with me. She did. We went to the cafeteria and began to talk. *I was straightforward in sharing that I had no idea of what to say to her, except that I received a calling from Jesus to become a nun.* She shared with me the basic information of age range, sacrifice, and formation for her own religious order. I was delighted to meet her.

---

[43] "The Easter Triduum begins with the evening Mass of the Lord's Supper on Holy Thursday, reaches its high point in the Easter Vigil, and closes with Evening Prayer on Easter Sunday." (U.S. Catholic Council of Bishops, "Eighteen Questions on the Paschal Triduum." *www.usccb.org/prayer-and-worship/liturgical-year-and-calendar/triduum/questions-and-answers*).

After Mass that evening, the entire congregation, with candles, followed at least sixty priests to the lower crypt of the church for Eucharistic Adoration at the shrine. This is the practice of adoring Jesus Christ in the stillness, in prayer, and in peace.

Within an hour, everyone departed except for seven Missionaries of Charity (Saint Teresa of Calcutta's sisters), two other lay women, and myself. I felt drawn to this order—another unexplainable phenomenon. I moved from my pew to sit closer to the sisters in the hopes of speaking with them; however, I knew it was not appropriate to talk during adoration, so I declined. I observed that they were patient, calm, and quiet angels of mercy. I admired them because they serve the suffering Christ every day, and do not desert him.

I wanted to stay with Jesus during his most difficult hours, and so I did. This was after his Last Supper with his disciples, after he washed their feet in an act of humility.

I was thinking to myself, "*Jesus, why are you drawing me to the Missionaries of Charity?*" I prayed the Rosary three times that night, a marathon for me. *At that moment I wished I had entered a convent when I was a younger woman, but quickly overcame that thought, knowing that had this happened, I never would have known my husband, amazing three sons, and their families.*

God knows what he is doing. He allowed me to be a wife, mother, and businesswoman, and to take these lessons learned and wisdom gained into prisons today, to work with men and women who genuinely want to become better versions of themselves, but do not know how to do this. I am grateful and humbled by this opportunity.

Jen, a spiritually-grounded Catholic, shared with me once that "When you open the door to let Jesus in, you cannot easily filter who will come through that door." What she was talking about were the influences of Satan to tempt me to stop following the calling from Jesus.

I am thankful my eyes are finally open and I am listening with the ears of my heart, to be more compassionate, listening to Jesus. I have become more aware of spiritual warfare and aware of the spiritual realm. I try to take every opportunity to make others aware of the forces of good and evil, and the fight for souls.

I love my faith journey with God, Jesus, our Blessed Mother Mary, my Guardian Angel, and all the angels and saints. I am grateful for all my blessings, gifts, and graces I receive every day. It is becoming so much easier to see God's hand at work. My heart, mind, and soul are open to receive the will of God, to act on his will, not mine.

Our "yes" as Catholic sisters is similar to, but not the same as the fiat, the "yes," of our Blessed Mother Mary, the mother of Jesus Christ. Following is her prayer after she said "yes" to the will of God for her.

Canticle of Mary (Luke 1:46-55)

My soul proclaims the greatness of the Lord,
my spirit rejoices in God my Savior
for he has looked with favor on his lowly servant.

From this day all generations will call me blessed:
the Almighty has done great things for me,
and holy is his Name.

He has mercy on those who fear him
in every generation.

He has shown the strength of his arm,
he has scattered the proud in their conceit.

He has cast down the mighty from their thrones,
and has lifted up the lowly.

He has filled the hungry with good things,
and the rich he has sent away empty.

He has come to the help of his servant Israel
for he has remembered his promise of mercy,
the promise he made to our fathers,
to Abraham and his children forever.

Glory to the Father, and to the Son,
and to the Holy Spirit,
as it was in the beginning, is now, and will be forever.

Amen

Mary was around the age of fourteen years old when the Angel Gabriel announced to her that she would be the mother of Jesus. Her strong faith in God kept her from being fearful of this and she was completely willing to comply with his will. She did not let Satan deter her from fulfilling God's will for her. She had no relations with a man, yet she would be with child, carrying God's only beloved son. "With God, all things are possible" (Lk. 1:26-38 and Mt. 19:16).

She endured a long journey on a donkey to Bethlehem and gave birth in a dirty, smelly stable. Even at that time, the evil one tried to set up an obstacle to interfere with this miraculous event, as they were not able to find suitable lodging. But God always wins in the end. Through his providence, he led them to a place for her to give birth, albeit I am sure the stable was not what they expected.

God's son was born to Mary and Joseph. He is the long-awaited Messiah.

A baby.

Questions for the reader to contemplate: Am I aware of the presence of good and evil and how it affects our lives? Do I know how to stay armored up against evil?

CHAPTER 5
SEARCHING FOR AN ORDER

Jesus told me to become a nun. I did not know how to proceed. I met with my priest, Father Brian, who coached me on the discernment process. He advised me to pray continually, to talk with Jesus and ask him to lead me where I was supposed to go. I needed to take my time with discernment though, and not be too hasty with my decisions.

There were no procedures manuals available for this. I wanted to follow through with what Jesus called me to do, but I did not know what to do. In my various careers, I had procedures manuals to follow, but not this time! And I did not know any religious sisters personally at the beginning of this journey who I could simply call to talk about this.

The journey involved an active search for an order who would take an older woman with pre-existing conditions of rheumatoid arthritis and fibromyalgia, two serious debilitating diseases. At the time I started this search, both diseases were controlled with medicine, yet the religious orders I approached still saw me as too much of a medical risk to accept, and were concerned I might not be able to do physical work.

In my research for religious orders to contact and visit, I looked for orders located in Georgia, as I knew that someday I would eventually live closer to family members there.

One of the church staff told me about *The Official Catholic Directory*[44] that all Catholic Churches usually have in their offices as a resource. This directory contains statistical and contact information. I copied the pages of the Atlanta Archdiocese to identify religious orders. Most of my contact was done by phone or email. I visited a few orders as well.

Mostly because of my age, then secondarily, my medical history, the traditional orders could not consider me, based upon their statutes. Another reason I was told I could not be accepted was that the younger and older generations do not normally mix too well, which is understandable. However, some orders have accepted older women. It is best to check directly with the order you are interested in joining.

Some categories of community types are:

➢ Apostolic/evangelical
➢ Missionary
➢ Contemplative
➢ Monastic
➢ Cloistered

Apostolic/evangelical, missionary, and contemplative were consistent with what Jesus told me on the day of my calling, to serve those in the world who are waiting for me. Monastic and cloistered were not options, as they typically do not serve the world; instead, their day is focused more on prayer and chores, although some monasteries interact with the public. Cloistered means that as a nun, I would not leave the convent to serve the world. Jesus told me to serve the suffering Christ, so being cloistered would not be an option for me.

There are web sites for those pursuing a calling to inquire about vocations. One place to start might be the U.S. Catholic

---

[44] To learn more, visit: *www.officialcatholicdirectory.com*.

Council of Bishops web site, www.usccb.org/beliefs-and-teachings/vocations.

Another resource is the Vicar of Religious in your diocese. This person can help guide the individual to find the path to take towards the specific calling of the person. Their contact information is usually on the diocese web site. If it is not listed, check with your church office staff to locate the contact information for you.

An important point that was made by a religious sister I met on my journey was that if a traditional order accepted me, and I was undergoing the first five years of formation with them, that I would not likely be released from formation to see my family, with few exceptions. This was important to consider since I am a mother and grandmother.

At this point, I still did not know where I was going on this journey.

It is difficult to make the transition from being self-serving to becoming self-less. I learned in formation that life is not about what I want. Even writing this book now seems vain to me, yet I must fulfill what Jesus asked me to do, because helping others with their spiritual journeys is a good fruit of the Holy Spirit.

I now understand the importance of writing this book. Sometime along the way, the realization set in, that I am not going to seek ways to make me happy any longer. Life becomes taking care of others and finding the kind of joy I found on the Jamaican mission trip.

There is a difference between temporary happiness of this world, and the lasting joy God provides.

My whole life was about to change. I did not know I would experience a kind of rebirth of myself with all the changes that would happen. I was thinking at that time, that in the *following* year after my calling and before I retired, that I would make changes, nothing too soon or too quick.

I thought, "Next year I will retire, sell the new house, and move to Georgia to live closer to family." But what about the calling? I still could not tell Jesus "no" because I had heard his voice for two years before the calling. *I knew him and what he was asking of me.*

I spoke to Father Brian before Mass soon after this thought of waiting for another year, not to retire right away. I shared with him what I was thinking of doing. He said, "What are you waiting for? How much money do you have to have?" He was right. There was no reason to delay the calling, and I did not need to continue earning a high income. *For what purpose?*

A short little piece of prose I came across that resonated with me about this:

If not us,
who?

If not here,
where?

If not now,
when?

If not for the Kingdom,
Why?

Dare the dream.[45]

About this time, I chatted with a very spiritual person, a Protestant who was recognized in his faith circles as a prophet. He also said he had been an exorcist. I shared my calling with him. He believed my purpose in life would be

---

[45] Based on a saying of Rabbi Hillel the Elder (110 BC to 10 AD) recorded in the *Mishna*, Pirkei Avot 1:14, quoted and paraphrased by countless people over the millennia since then.

an intercessor with prayer and fasting, and that I would work alongside a priest to rid people of demons. *My response to that was, "Why would God pick me for that?"* I still have not done this kind of work, and I am not contemplating doing this. However, if God should tell me to do this type of ministry someday, I will.

I merely have to be patient, persevere, enjoy the journey, not tell God what to do, and help people along the way.

The next step of the journey was to go to my first mini-retreat on the weekend. I attended quite a few of these. The retreats were on Saturday mornings and led by a very gifted retreat leader, Trish. She would engage our thinking in ways we never considered. This was another effective way to grow spiritually on my journey, contemplating things I had never considered.

Once we know what God's will is for us, by discerning (praying) what he is calling us to do, his plan will begin to play out. It may not happen overnight though. We have to be patient and persevere through the process, because "God's timing is not our timing" (2 Pet. 3:8-9).

In talking with my Aunt Patsy, she shared with me her belief that if I pray for patience in searching for an order, that God will give me situations to test my patience. She is a special mentor in my life, solid in her Catholic faith, and she watches over all of her family and extended family. She was correct. Searching for an order tried my patience. This search was frustrating because it was slow with many dead ends. I wanted to fulfill the calling, but I could not do this until I found the order I would belong to.

Each person's discerning is different, because each calling and individual is unique.

Additionally, God gives us signs, or confirmations, that we are on the right track *if* our eyes are open to see them. I have received many confirmations from him that I am doing what he wants me to do. For example, almost every day, he places someone in front of me, a stranger who wants to inquire or share their faith. I know this is God's doing. Wearing the habit and veil in public has a lot to do with it as well. Every time I go into a grocery store to get a few groceries, it can take me awhile because of the conversations that take place. The joyful surprise, though, is that these confirmations fulfill my calling and fill me with joy.

For nearly nine months, I searched for an order of Catholic sisters to consider accepting me, but to no avail. I lost hope and began to doubt my calling, though I should not have. During another retreat, the retreat leader gave us a beautiful writing to reflect upon:

The Slow Work of God[46]

Above all, trust in the slow work of God.
We are quite naturally impatient in everything
to reach the end without delay.
We should like to skip the intermediate stages.
We are impatient of being on the way to something
unknown, something new.
And yet it is the law of all progress that it is made
by passing through some stages of instability,
and that it may take a very long time.

And so I think it is with you;
your ideas mature gradually—let them grow,
let them shape themselves, without undue haste.
Don't try to force them on, as though you could be today

---

[46] Pierre Teilhard de Chardin, *The Making of a Mind: Letters from a Soldier-Priest 1914-1919* (New York: Harper & Row, 1961), 57.

what time (that is to say, grace and circumstances
acting on our own good will) will make of you tomorrow.

Only God could say what this new spirit
gradually forming within you will be.
Give our Lord the benefit of believing
that his hand is leading you,
and accept the anxiety of feeling yourself
in suspense and incomplete.

by Pierre Teilhard de Chardin

I received wonderful news during this period of time
though. During March-May 2011, I suffered from daily pain
which was the result of rheumatoid arthritis and fibromyalgia
flareups.

*This was when I prayed to God, with all of my being, that
"If you will just take away these diseases, I will do whatever you
want for the rest of my life."*

In June 2011, during a routine rheumatology appointment,
the rheumatologist suggested that my rheumatoid arthritis
factor be tested (blood work). The results came back negative.
The doctor and I were surprised. *Then I prayed I would remain
in remission to allow me to fully serve others who suffer, if this
was compatible with God's will for me.*

After I received the negative blood test, and during that
same month in June, I was sitting in a small discussion group
at a retreat center with five other people. We were asked by the
retreat leader to share our journeys of faith with each other.

There was a woman who sat next to me whom I had
never seen before at our retreats, and after that day, I never
saw her at retreats again. Was she God's messenger for me?
I think so.

God then did what he does so well. He orchestrated an
incredible, beautiful moment.

After I shared my pitiful journey with the group about not finding an order that would take me, the woman sitting next to me turned towards me to say, "You need to talk to Sister Lillian." I said, "Ok." They were friends. She gave me sister's contact information. As I wrote down her phone number, I thought to myself that this would be another rejection. Convinced of this, I did not even bother to contact this sister for two months. I was not in a hurry because I had lost hope and I doubted the calling.

What are the odds that I would meet someone who was friends with a sister of an association of sisters who are called late-in-life? It could have happened that this woman at the retreat had not been listening to me in the small group circle either. But she was listening. She knew, after listening to me, that I should contact this sister. God orchestrated this. I did not realize it at the time. It is always easier to look back to see things more clearly. *There are no coincidences.*

Doubting the calling was a test of my faith. How strong was my faith? I knew his voice, no question about that. I know what he said. No doubt there. Why was I no longer motivated to move forward with this calling?

I am one who typically follows through, though. I called Sister Lillian in August 2011, one year after the calling. Of course, I had many questions for her. These are just a few:

How long is formation?
Do I have to sell my house?
Can I talk with my family during formation?
When would I start formation?
Where do I do formation?
Do we take vows? What are they?
What are the costs associated with formation?
Do we wear a habit?
What is formation, and what happens during this time?
What happens after formation?

What if I have a medical condition controlled with medicine?

Much to my surprise, during the phone call, I felt completely welcomed by this sister. None of the questions I asked resulted in "no." I was elated and anxious at the same time. Much like the day of the calling, I felt overwhelmed by the phone call with Sister Lillian. Why? I realized that it was a possibility that my life was about to change in many drastic ways.

The sister invited me to visit her and two other sisters in Lockhart, Texas. These visits are called come-and-see visits. The purpose of the visit is for the sisters of the association, and the potential candidate herself, to get to know each other, to see if she might be a good fit for the association, and for her to discern if the association is the right fit for her.

I decided to visit the sisters during September 1-6, 2011. I did not share this with friends, family, or my supervisor. I just booked a flight and went. I was drawn by some unexplainable force. Was the force God himself? The spontaneous decision to visit religious sisters without telling anyone what I was doing, was yet another illogical and unreasonable action on my part.

I was extremely nervous about visiting the sisters. This seemed to be a huge leap of faith as I was uncertain of many things. *Thirty-three* minutes before the plane landed in Austin, Texas, the pilot said over the intercom, "Ladies and gentlemen, we will be landing in thirty-three minutes (then gave the weather, etc.)." I began to laugh out loud, and I am sure no one around me knew why. You see, in Christian circles, we see instances of numerology sometimes, especially with the number three. In this case, thirty-three is the age Jesus was crucified.

I recognized that God was giving me a sign that everything was going to be okay. The reference to Jesus was a reminder that he was walking with me on this journey. I breathed a sigh of relief when I heard the pilot. And laughing releases tension, naturally, which is exactly what I needed, as it took away my fear.

When I was at the baggage claim, again, I had huge anxiety. Why? I realized that I would meet the sisters very soon. Then what? Fear of the unknown is the worst. I thought to myself that it was not too late to leave without meeting them, because they did not know what I looked like. It was tempting! But I did not leave.

Two sisters, Sister Lillian and Sister John Mary, greeted me at the baggage claim. They were so welcoming and full of smiles and love. I felt at ease. Once we got to the car, I met the driver, Sister Rita, who was also very friendly.

We drove to their location in a tiny town south of Austin - Lockhart, Texas, home of the best barbecue in the world, and a place of numerous movie productions.

We had a lovely, informative, five-day visit with each other, and I was invited to return, with the possibility of joining the association of sisters. During this visit, I participated with the sisters by going with them to daily Mass and visiting the sick and dying. I also prayed the *Divine Office*[47] with them during their morning, evening, and night prayers.

On September 26, 2011, I submitted my retirement application to the agency. Just before this, I saw that my agency was offering early retirements, giving active employees the opportunity to retire early with an incentive bonus if they met certain criteria, which I did. God was at work again,

---

[47] *Christian Prayer: The Liturgy of the Hours*, English Translation Prepared by the International Commission on English in the Liturgy, Catholic Book Publishing Co. New York, 1976.

arranging things for me so I could easily transition from employment to formation, to become a sister. Unbelievable.

God has a way of opening doors even when we do not ask him to.

On October 14, 2011, I submitted the formal application to the association of sisters. Before the association accepted me, I attended another Saturday retreat. I was already changing from the inside out, mostly from the Jamaican mission trip, returning to the church to receive the Eucharist (Jesus Christ), listening to Jesus every day, and reading *Jesus Calling*,[48] a Christian daily devotional. At this retreat, while in a reflective, meditative and prayerful mode, I created this little prayer:

> Dear God, help me learn how to deliver your message. Give me the strength and wisdom to minister in the ways you have planned for me. Let me wash their feet with my tears, and dry their feet with my hair. It is out of my sins that I have been forgiven, that I am learning to show great love. My faith has saved me, and I now go in peace.

I thought I was going to have to wait a long time to start formation. There were no other orders, congregations, or associations calling or writing to me, showing an interest. During this time, I decided that if I was not accepted by the Eudist Servants of the Eleventh Hour, that I would simply retire and move to Georgia, to live closer to my family.

While I waited to be accepted to start formation with the Eudist Servants, a good friend of mine, who has since become a sister with our association, Sister Dolores, invited me to attend a Cursillo[49] weekend in October 2011. Cursillo

---

[48] Sarah Young, *Jesus Calling* (Nashville, Tennessee: Thomas Nelson, 2004).

[49] To learn more, visit *www.natl-cursillo.org.*

events take place all over the world. Your local Catholic Church probably already has people who are actively involved in Cursillo. It was a beautiful weekend of Christian fellowship, prayer, meditation, reflection, Mass, singing hymns, wonderful food, and so much more.

Our housing for that weekend was lodging in bunk houses. I remember my experience well. I shared with the other attendees at the end of the weekend that now I have a little bit of an idea of what it feels like to sleep in a homeless shelter. Why? The bunkhouse contained about fifteen women, all in bunk beds. I am a light sleeper. I heard snoring all night long, so I did not get a good night's rest that weekend. Because it was a bunk house, there was very little privacy and only one shower.

What was great about this experience, though, were the spiritual things we all had in common. It was good to share with others about where we were on our journeys. I had also never felt the level of love and caring before, that we all received that weekend.

Everyone working on the Cursillo team made an effort to make each new person feel loved. I had a restrictive diet and the team made sure my diet was satisfied. I was amazed at how caring all of them were. The food was incredible. No one went hungry that weekend.

On November 4, 2011, I received a call from a very spiritual woman, Mary Bernadette, who had befriended me at the Saturday retreats. She is deceased now, but she was the most prayerful woman I have ever met. She shared that she would begin prayer at 3:00 a.m. every morning, and end at 11:00 a.m. She said she would see the Gospels of the Bible play out in front of her while she prayed. And she said she would bleed from her temple area when she prayed ardently. She and I experienced an unexplained mystical event together that evening. I will go into further detail about this in a later chapter, "Collection of Personal Stories." The story is titled *Precious Blood Daily Devotional*. It is important to at least mention that this special event occurred at this time before I retired and entered formation, and it was another confirmation of God calling me to serve.

On November 30, 2011, I retired from the federal government. My assistant chief organized a nice retirement party. She reached out to my sons to ask if they could attend. None of them lived close to me and all of them worked. My oldest son, an Air Force Pilot, was coincidentally (there's that word again) flying into Joint Base Andrews, Maryland, and was within driving distance of my office, but I did not know this before the retirement party took place. When I saw my son, my maternal instincts kicked in because I had tears of joy when I saw him at the party. I did not think anyone would be able to attend because everyone lived so far away.

God has a way of making extraordinary things happen when we least expect it. He already knows the desires of our hearts, and he knew how much it meant for me to have my family at my retirement gathering.

Questions for the reader to contemplate: If I received a calling today, how would I pursue it? Who would I contact? What will I ask? What will my journey be? Is God calling me? Am I allowing the evil one to be an obstacle? Do I doubt the calling? How do I prepare to make drastic changes?

CHAPTER 6
EUDIST SERVANTS OF THE ELEVENTH HOUR

⸙

On October 29, 2011, I received a call, asking if I would like to enter formation with the Eudist Servants of the Eleventh Hour, beginning formation in April 2012. I said, "yes!" I was overjoyed.

In the next chapter, I will share more on the formation process itself. Here, I will cover details about this association of sisters who are called late in life.

Mother Antonia Brenner, formerly known as Mary Clarke, lived a life of privilege in Beverly Hills, California. She was born to affluent parents who helped the poor, both domestically and internationally. Serving the poor was instilled in Mary at an early age. She was driven to continue to serve those who suffer as she grew older.

A more detailed account of Mother Antonia's life and ministries is found in *The Prison Angel*.[50] It is a quick and easy read and can be purchased at our association's web site, *www.eudistservants.org*.

---

[50] Mary Jordan & Kevin Sullivan, *The Prison Angel* (New York: The Penguin Press, 2006).

She married and divorced twice and became the mother of eight children. One child died shortly after birth. After twenty-five years of marriage and divorce, and when most of her children were out of the house, she found herself *not* wholly content with just raising a family any longer, and she was drawn to prison ministry.

"In a period of just a few years, she divorced, sold her home and possessions, and began to serve full time the prisoners at La Mesa penitentiary in Tijuana, Mexico, and with permission to take private vows, she put on a religious habit. After a year, her service to prisoners came to the attention of Bishop Juan Jesus Posadas of Tijuana and Bishop Leo Maher of neighboring San Diego. She was officially welcomed and blessed by both Bishops: Bishop Maher made her an auxiliary to him while Bishop Posadas made her an auxiliary Mercedarian, an order which has a special devotion to prisoners. At age fifty, she had become a sister. At the La Mesa penitentiary, she lived in a 10' x 10' concrete room with a cot as her bed, and with a Bible and Spanish dictionary nearby. Sister Antonia provided not only spiritual guidance to the guards and inmates, but continued to help with basic material comforts for prisoners such as blankets, toiletries and medicines."[51]

Mother Antonia lived in the Tijuana penitentiary for over thirty years, yet never committed a crime. She befriended everyone, including the inmates, guards, infirmary staff, and wardens. She was greatly loved and highly respected by everyone who met her because of her genuine love for others, no matter what their crimes and sins were.

---

[51] "Biography of Mother Antonia Brenner," accessed on Jan. 25, 2021. *www.eudistservants.org/biography-of-mother-antonia-brenner.*

She also befriended St. Teresa of Calcutta (formerly known as Mother Teresa).

Mother Antonia Brenner with St. Teresa of Calcutta

Author Heather King gives an account of mother in this way: "Petite, indefatigable in her black and white habit, she lived as one of the inmates, in a ten-by-ten cell. She ate the same prison fare and, with the members of her flock, lined up for morning roll call."[52]

Heather adds that, "In a 1982 interview with the Los Angeles Times, Brenner said, 'Something happened to me when I saw men behind bars…When I left, I thought a lot about the men. When it was cold, I wondered if the men were warm; when it was raining, if they had shelter. I wondered if they had medicine and how their families were doing… You know, when I returned to the prison to live, I felt as if I'd come home.'"[53]

Mother Antonia stayed connected with her family members as she made these drastic changes to her life, to

---

[52] *Magnificat, December 2016, vol. 18, no. 10* (Yonkers, New York: Magnificat), 44.
[53] *Ibid.*

serve the least of her brothers and sisters. Called to serve in a specific way, she visited the imprisoned.

Jesus told us to visit those in prison (Mt. 25:35-45). The content of these lines of scripture were not suggestions.

In 2003, she expanded her ministry by establishing a private association of the faithful of consecrated sisters: the Eudist Servants of the Eleventh Hour, of which I am now a part of. Established in Tijuana, Mexico, and under the Bishop of Tijuana (in later years, the position of Bishop would become Archbishop), our charism is mercy, working in ministries of mercy; however, our primary ministry is prison ministry.

Every sister is expected to work in prison ministry wherever she resides, as this is the foundation of Mother Antonia's ministry. If a sister is not able to gain access to work in an incarcerated facility in her area, she may work in other ministries of mercy. Most of our sisters work in ministries without pay; however, some must continue to earn income. Therefore, we are allowed to be employed to sustain ourselves, but only in ministries of mercy. And we must work with the least of our brothers and sisters in-person, if this is possible.

Private associations of the faithful are a category under Canon Law.[54] We are not a traditional order. We are consecrated sisters, not cloistered nuns. Jesus told me specifically to become a nun; however, I never became a nun, per se, because he also told me on the day of my calling to serve those who suffer. We cannot serve those who suffer if we are cloistered as nuns; instead, we serve those who suffer, as sisters.

---

[54] To learn more, go to *www.vatican.va/archive/cod-iuris-canonici/cic_index_ en.html*. Additionally, a simple summary of the differences between nuns and sisters is: *www.canonlawmadeeasy.com/2009/03/19/whats-the-difference-between- sisters-and-nuns*.

I am honored to wear the habit and veil every day in public as this is one way God is using me to bring others to the cross. For example, as I walk through an airport, department store, or parking lot, there are many people present. Just seeing a sister in a habit may cause a person to ponder on their existence, purpose in life, and their relationship with God. And when they stop to pray with me, or talk about their faith, or sorrow, for example, it is an honor to be present with them, helping them in their journey of faith.

We follow the spirituality of Saint John Eudes and Mother Antonia Brenner. I will share more about this in the next chapter on the formation of our sisters.

At one point during this time, I doubted my path to become a sister with the Eudist Servants, because Jesus said to become a nun, and these sisters were technically not nuns. After some deliberation, I finally realized what was important was to focus on the fruit of the Holy Spirit, which is the work that we do.

I needed to recognize that the work we do of serving those who suffer was far more important than whether we were technically sisters or nuns.

I wanted to be sure I was not disobeying what Jesus told me to do specifically, to become a nun. After much prayer and sharing in Christian fellowship with others, I became confident I was on the right path to become a Eudist Servant. God showed me the beautiful and rewarding work of prison ministry, something I never dreamed I would consider. *How could I turn my back on that after he showed this suffering to me? How could I say "no" to serving the suffering Christ when I knew it was God showing me this?"*

Knowing Jesus, and serving him, "the suffering Christ," is how we come to understand our purpose in life.

We have a unique organization of sisters due to the history of our association, including the reasons we wear the habit and veil. We wear this attire as a Catholic witness to others, and for security reasons in prisons.

Sister John Mary Schweikardt tending to a man's foot in front of the Tijuana formation house, Casa Corazon de Maria - 2015

Our prayer life consists of praying the *Divine Office*[55] in the morning, evening, and at night. When we are in the presence of another sister, we pray together. We also attend daily Mass, pray the Divine Mercy Chaplet and Rosary, attend retreats, go to confession, and Eucharistic Adoration. Sisters may also include daily devotionals and novenas in their daily prayers. Bible study and review of the *Catechism of the Catholic Church* should be visited routinely.

Our vows of poverty, chastity, obedience, and divine love are renewed every year in Tijuana, Mexico. Each year all the

---

[55] *Christian Prayer: The Liturgy of the Hours*, English Translation Prepared by the International Commission on English in the Liturgy, Catholic Book Publishing Co. New York, 1976.

sisters from the United States and Mexico come together to renew vows, participate in the assembly meeting, and experience a retreat together. We look forward to this very much, spending time with our fellow sisters, catching up, and sharing in Catholic fellowship with one another. It is a rich experience filled with love, peace, and joy.

A little side note on the below picture of Sister Elaine and me, playing basketball, is that I do not know how to play basketball, but she does. We needed a break from developing updates to our association statutes, so we tossed the ball around in the street, without any rules, and a lot of laughter! Sisterhood can be so much fun.

Playing basketball with Sister Elaine in
Tijuana – 2017
(Picture taken by Debbie Schweikardt –
Sister John Mary's daughter)

Those of us who travel from the United States, fly to the San Diego airport where a sister picks us up, then we drive over the U.S - Mexico border, to our location in Tijuana. Much of the city is at the level of a third world country because of the extreme poverty that exists there. It is a place of hardship, and there are very few safety nets like we see in the United States through the generous help of local churches and faith-based charity organizations like St. Vincent de Paul Society.[56]

The services of the Red Cross in Tijuana are available to the sisters. Once I was developing a sinus infection and bronchitis, and my sisters took me to the Red Cross. There was a communication barrier because I do not speak Spanish, and I could not convey my symptoms. Finally, the third doctor to see me understood English. He ordered a chest x-ray, prescribed medicine, and I was on my way.

Another time, I came down with a sinus infection, the sisters took me to see the local doctor. It cost $3.00 for a doctor's visit! He prescribed the medicine, then we went next door to the pharmacy, to purchase the medication. The cost of the medicine was a surprise because Tijuana does not have the medical insurance we are used to, where our premiums cover most of the cost of prescriptions. My prescriptions are typically quite low in price, but not that time.

Any sister or candidate who has been sick while they were in Tijuana, has gotten the help they needed, whether it was in Tijuana, or in the United States, depending upon what the medical issue was. Our sisters take care of one another while we are in Tijuana. This may be mainly because most of us are mothers and grandmothers and we have a lot of experience tending to others! And currently we have two new sisters who are a doctor, Sister Lourdes, and a nurse, Sister Ann Gertrude, who are a delight to have in our association.

On this journey to become a sister, there are many changes to make, then adjust to. Remember the title of the

---

[56] For more information on this faith-based charity, see the national website, *www.svdpusa.org*, and in Georgia, *www.svdpgeorgia.org*.

first chapter in this book: *You Are Who You Aren't?* The essence of becoming who God is waiting for us to become, is merely choosing to change in many ways. These changes happen internally and externally as we go along on the journey, becoming what he wants us to be.

A little healthy fear is okay at first, while striving to make these changes, but every person who says "yes" to the Lord will eventually have to muster the courage that is needed to move forward, one day at a time.

God gives us the grace we need to change.

When I met my spiritual director, Father Richard Wise, for the first time, and I informed him of this association of sisters, his comment was, "I believe this is going to be the future of the church." He was referring to associations of the faithful. The basis of his comment was that so many of the traditional orders have greatly diminished in number over the years; however, some are still flourishing.

Father Wise is wise.

Mother Antonia passed away on October 13, 2013, yet her sisters continue to work in Mexico and the United States. The sisters in Tijuana are always in need of donations[57] to buy much-needed supplies to help the least of our brothers and sisters, serving the prisoners, their families, and the marginalized.

---

[57] Donations to help prisoners and their families, and the poor, may be made at our website, *www.eudistservants.org*.

Sisters waiting for Mass to begin in the new chapel of
Casa Corazon de Jesus – 2017.[58]

As a side note, the voluminous and inspirational writings
of Saint John Eudes, our patron saint, were submitted by
the Bishops' Conference of France to the Vatican for
consideration to become a Doctor of The Church. As of this
writing, we patiently await their decision.

> *Questions for the reader to contemplate: If I have a calling to
> serve the least of my brothers and sisters, am I being called to
> serve as a priest, deacon, brother, sister, or lay person? Is God
> asking me to move out of my comfort zone, to make drastic
> changes in my life? Is there anything I need to be free of in
> order to serve those who suffer?*

---

[58] This much-needed chapel was built with benefactor donations specifically
dedicated to the building of the new chapel, with the vision and oversight of
Sister Judith Krantz, General Leader at that time. A special collection was made
for this effort. No funds were used from the donations collected for the prisoners,
their families, and the marginalized.

CHAPTER 7
FORMAL DISCERNMENT, FORMATION, AND PRAYER

O n April 3, 2012, I arrived in Lockhart, Texas, for formal discernment and formation with the Eudist Servants of the Eleventh Hour.

As I was driving through Atlanta, I decided to stop at the archdiocese chancery to say hello to Sally, a person who had helped me previously with my search for religious orders. I wanted to let her know that I was on my way to join an association of the faithful, to enter formation in Texas.

Daily Mass was about to begin in the St. Dominic chapel. The archbishop and four priests concelebrated Mass. Remember the archbishop who celebrated Midnight Mass, where I saw Jesus move on the cross with my two friends? This was the same archbishop. After Mass, I told him I was on my way to begin formation to become a Catholic sister. He said, "Oh, I am so happy for you!" He squinted his eyes as he said this, with a huge smile on his face. I asked him for his blessing. He was happy to do so. Then I said goodbye and continued the drive to Texas.

The day after I arrived in Texas to begin formation, I became sick with the worst migraine headache I have ever had, with nausea and vomiting. The sisters took me to the

Luling, Texas, hospital emergency room, about a thirty-minute drive. The doctor said I had cedar fever. Pollen from the cedar trees caused an unbearable migraine headache. It probably did not help that I had driven through other active pollen regions of the country before arriving in Texas, because all these different regions had high pollen counts too. I was admitted to the hospital and was there for several days. The doctor gave me medicine that knocked me out.

Mysteriously, that night I was awakened to find a young man with dark hair who sat next to my bed, in the darkness. He seemed to be watching me sleep. He did not say anything to me, and I did not speak to him. It seemed as though he was watching over me as an angel would. I never saw him again. *And when I asked the nurses the next day about him, they did not know anyone by that description.* I was discharged, grateful for their help.

There were two of us who began formation at the same time, Sister San Juanita and myself. Women who are considered for acceptance in the Eudist Servants must be (1) able to start formation between the ages of 45 and 65 years old, (2) financially self-sufficient, (3) in good health (medical conditions that can be managed with medicine) and (4) able to provide for their own medical insurance. The formation directress who screens possible candidates may also have other criteria that needs to be addressed as well, and as she feels is necessary.[59]

The formation house mother, Sister Lillian, received all the required paperwork before we arrived, including (1) letter from the pastor, (2) letter from the doctor, (3) letter from the

---

[59] Contained within this chapter are many of the specifics of our particular association of the faithful. Some of the details vary from one organization to another, and depending upon what type of organization a person is considering joining.

psychiatrist or pastor, and (4) any other documentation, as requested.

At that time, the annulment was not required for a divorced woman to enter formation, but today it is required. Any woman who begins formation with our association today must submit her approved annulment letter from the Tribunal *before* starting formation.

My situation with the annulment was complicated. I filed my application for an annulment to my previous diocese soon after the calling in 2010 and before starting formation. The answer came in the middle of formation that the Tribunal denied my request.

Devastated, I met with the Austin Diocese Tribunal Vicar since I was in formation in the Austin diocese. He said I definitely had a case for an annulment because I was engaged at 17 and married at 19, both very young ages. The case was based on the category of immaturity, and there was no pre-marriage counseling provided by my church in 1972, the year we became engaged.

The Vicar's advice was to file a new application through the Austin diocese, since I was living in that diocese for part of my formation. Later my ex-husband passed away unexpectedly from congestive heart failure after I finished formation, and before the second annulment application had been fully processed. Since I never remarried, I was then considered a widow in the eyes of the Catholic Church. The annulment was no longer necessary.

We began our formal discernment, followed by formation.

What is discernment? This can be defined in several ways. Generally, from a Christian perspective, discernment is judging, based upon Holy Scripture, what is right and wrong, and knowing the difference, as it is applied to our daily situations. A Christian who is mature in their faith knows the difference, using the teachings of Jesus Christ in the Bible.

Discernment is also a term that can be used to apply to the decision of whether a candidate should remain with an association of sisters. The first three months are for the candidate and the association to determine, through discernment, if they are a good match for one another. How is the candidate adjusting to community life? Is the candidate able to do the work of the mission? Is the candidate able to learn how to pray the *Divine Office*[60] with the community? Is the candidate able to adapt to communal living and the ministries? These are only a few questions that need to be answered at the end of the first three months, to determine if the candidate should proceed to formation.

Additionally, after sisters make their vows, discernment remains a daily practice as something a sister does for the rest of her life, given situations that are presented to her. A vowed sister will also follow the teachings of our patron saint, Saint John Eudes, Mother Antonia, and other writings given to her during formation. After a sister makes her vows, she should seek out the help of a spiritual director to assist with her spiritual journey, going forward.

Another important piece of advice I was given at this time by the priest of the local Catholic Church was that because I am such an analytical person, I needed to change. I needed to merely let go and follow the leader. Also, I needed *not* to offer advice unless I was asked. Instead of trying to fix things, I needed to do what was expected of me. This was challenging for someone like me, who came into formation as a retired manager.

---

[60] *Christian Prayer: The Liturgy of the Hours*, English Translation Prepared by the International Commission on English in the Liturgy, Catholic Book Publishing Co. New York, 1976.

Most importantly, I needed to learn humility.

When a middle-aged person is used to being in charge, it can be challenging to let go. This change is necessary when we strive to become better versions of ourselves and to learn how to humble ourselves. It is more peaceful this way as well.

This transformation of the candidate is to learn that life is not about her. Life is about who she needs to serve—her focus changes to them, and life is no longer about her.

Once a candidate becomes a vowed sister, she has a voice in the annual assembly meeting. Until then, it is best to adhere to the community guidelines, and offer advice only when asked. This may seem like a drastic change, but in the broad view of the calling, having a voice in matters is *not* what is most important on a journey to become consecrated. However, if suggestions or opinions are requested, by all means, offer them.

At the end of three months of formal discernment, a determination is made about whether the candidate will be allowed to begin formation. The candidate also discerns at this time, if they are certain this is the path for them. It is a mutual agreement to proceed.

Formation with our association is mostly the spiritual forming of the candidate and lasts for six months or more, depending upon her developmental needs. After she makes her first vows,[61] she is required to serve in Tijuana for one year, continuing her individual formation. She will make many internal and external changes. She continues to refer to the resources she was given during formation. She learns the ways of the sisters, continues

---

[61] The sisters of our association of the faithful make temporary vows. "First vows" means it is the first time we make our vows. In successive years, we renew our vows annually. Our procedure of making vows differs from that of a traditional order which has more than one level of vows.

her ministries alongside the sisters, and under the tutelage of the formation directress.

Our formation directress gave us a beautiful prayer.

A Journey

Father,
I can never find my own way to
the high peak of your love, but
I know you can show me the way.
The way that Jesus walked.
I hear your voice calling to my
soul, "Rise and walk with me to
a new place."
Today, I begin a journey that
will lead me deeper into your love.

Amen (author unknown)

Our daily schedule was structured, praying the *Divine Office*[62] in the morning, evening, and at night. We also prayed the Angelus prayer at noon and the Divine Mercy Chaplet at 3:00 pm. We attended daily Mass.

Our ministries included prison ministry, working with women at a GEO-run incarcerated facility in Lockhart, Texas, becoming Extraordinary Ministers to bring the Eucharist to people who were homebound, visiting two nursing homes, helping at Alcoholics Anonymous meetings, Saint Vincent de Paul Society ministry, lector, leading the Rosary, Sacristan, and Catechism teacher.

---

[62] *Christian Prayer: The Liturgy of the Hours*, English Translation Prepared by the International Commission on English in the Liturgy, Catholic Book Publishing Co. New York, 1976.

Chores included grocery shopping, cooking, and cleaning. Any spare time we had was our personal time. If we wanted to go somewhere, we were asked to go in twos, and had to let someone know where we were going. Of course, if we had a request to travel, we would request permission from the formation house mother or formation directress first. These rules were to learn obedience, and also to be safe.

Living in a religious community is part of formation and requires some adjustment. We are different personalities and come from different walks in life. This involves change on everyone's part, requiring patience and perseverance, especially since we are middle-aged women. We come into formation with experience as mothers, grandmothers, and women with careers. This is one way we are different than the traditional orders of women, who begin formation in their twenties.

At the beginning of formation, we were also given two prayer cards that we use at the beginning of morning prayer, and before we pray the *Divine Office*.[63] The first prayer is:

Prayer to the Holy Spirit[64]

Come, Holy Spirit, fill my heart with your holy gifts.

Let my weakness be penetrated with your strength this very day that I may fulfill the duties of my state in life conscientiously, that I may do what is right and just.

Let my charity be such as to offend no one and hurt no one's feelings; so generous as to pardon sincerely any wrong done to me.

---

[63] *Christian Prayer: The Liturgy of the Hours*, English Translation Prepared by the International Commission on English in the Liturgy, Catholic Book Publishing Co. New York, 1976.

[64] Imprimatur: Samuel Cardinal Stritch, Archbishop of Chicago.

Assist me in all the trials of life, enlighten me in my ignorance, advise me in my doubts, strengthen my weakness, help me in all needs and embarrassment, protect me in temptations and console me in all afflictions.

Graciously hear me, Oh Holy Spirit, and pour your light into my heart, my soul and my mind. Assist me to live a holy life and to grow in goodness and grace.

Amen

Another prayer we say every morning is what we lovingly refer to as the Mother Antonia prayer, as these are her words:

Good Morning Dear Lord,[65]

Thank you for the precious gift
You have given me this morning–
my life-to live fully and joyfully
one more day! Please give me the
grace to be kind and patient today
that I may see beyond worldly
appearances, so that I may
encounter your holy presence
in each person I meet.

Close my ears dear Father to all
gossip. Seal my lips to all
judgments and criticisms that my
words will only bless all about
me and warm the coldest heart.

Let my actions be so just, my
feelings be so tender, my conduct
be so humble and true to
your will that throughout this
day I will be a reflection of

---

[65] Mother Antonia Brenner, Eudist Servants of the Eleventh Hour.

your heavenly mercy and love.

Amen

While I was in formation, I brought others along with me on the journey via emails. I did this because at the beginning of the Cursillo *Pilgrim's Guide* book,[66] I was reminded that this formation phase of my life is also a pilgrimage, and to bring my brothers and sisters along with me. For a while, and as I had time, I sent an email to my family and friends to share experiences with them, so they would have an idea of what the journey entailed; however, I honestly did not have the time to share all the details of the journey.

At one point, I became discouraged, sad, and feeling as though I did not belong in the community. Yet Jesus called me to become a nun. What was I supposed to do? I knew his voice. I went to perpetual Eucharistic Adoration at the Catholic Church in Buda, Texas, not far from where we lived. We were encouraged to go to adoration especially when we were experiencing difficult times, and to enter into centered prayer, reflection, and meditation.

I had a history of communicating with the Holy Spirit, Jesus, nearly every day. I heard God only once before I started formation. He had a stern voice and was brief in speaking with me. But I never heard Mary until that day in perpetual adoration. I knelt to pray in the chapel, assuming I would hear Jesus, as I normally did.

Whenever I heard any of them, they were not audible voices, and what they said was always good, pertinent to current issues, and helpful.

The moment my knees hit the kneeler, I heard the most beautiful feminine voice I had ever heard in my life. *I knew it was Our Blessed Mother Mary. She said, "You will have to*

---

[66] To learn more, visit *www.natl-cursillo.org*.

endure a while longer." I had not even begun to pray, when I heard this voice. I felt a huge sense of relief when I heard these words. I knew everything was going to be okay from that moment going forward. Everything became easier, just knowing that God, Jesus, and Mary were walking with me on this journey.

Later, after I became a sister, I joined a Marian Movement of Priests[67] prayer group, where the participants pray the Rosary, and reflect upon the messages of Our Blessed Mother Mary to Father Don Stefano Gobbi. This brought me closer to Mary. The group continues to be led by Meg and Tony Jatcko at my church, who are devoted to the Blessed Mother. Joining a prayer group of any kind helps to keep Christians spiritually grounded in the faith. "Where two or more are gathered, there am I in the midst of them" (Mt. 18:20).

In the formation process to become a sister, I was learning to be open to trusting God more.

Every week during formation, we were given assigned reading. We met to discuss what we read and studied. I enjoyed these meetings because I learned from the sisters, and the other candidate as well.

Especially insightful works on the spirituality of Saint John Eudes can be found at the *www.eudistsusa.org web site.* My favorite selection, *In All Things, The Will of God,*[68] contains compassionate letters of Saint John Eudes to others in their time of need. This book gives us a glimpse of who this saint was, a kind and charitable priest. He was also known for establishing seminaries and rescuing women of ill repute to

---

[67] To learn more, *visit www.mmp-usa.net.* Also see *The Spiritual Power of My Cenacles* by the Marian Movement of Priests National Headquarters-USA, 2000. See especially page 5, *The Cenacles-Their Spiritual Benefits and Power.*

[68] Bishop Clément Guillon, *In All Things, The Will of God,* trans. Louis Levesque (Solana Beach, California: Eudist Press, 2019).

help them learn how to live a better life. His feast day on the church liturgical calendar is August 19th.

Additionally, a set of writings by Saint John Eudes, referred to as the Eudist Prayerbook Series, can be purchased on *www.amazon.com*. The five volumes are: *Heart of the Holy Family*, *More Than Just 50 Beads*, *A Holy Week Every Week*, *34 Flames of Divine Love*, and *On the Threshold of Life*. These resources were brilliantly developed, yet easy and practical to use for anyone who wishes to deepen their spirituality. They are now being used as additional resources in the formation of candidates to become Catholic sisters with our association.

In August 2012, the time came to receive our first habits. I remember the first time I put on the dress of the habit, which is worn first, under the scapular (outer layer). I felt a warmth that went through my body immediately after I put it on. I knew it was the Holy Spirit of God. I cried. *They were tears of joy, not sadness. The tears came because of all I had been through up to that point, making drastic changes in my life to become what God wanted me to be and to do.*

Another beautiful prayer we were given during formation:

The Prayer of Saint Francis

Lord, make me an instrument of your peace;
Where there is hatred, let me sow love;
Where there is injury, pardon;
Where there is doubt, faith;
Where there is despair, hope;
Where there is darkness, light
And where there is sadness, joy.

Oh Divine Master,
Grant that I may not so much seek to be
Consoled as to console;

To be understood, as to understand;
To be loved, as to love;
For it is in giving that we receive,
It is in pardoning that we are pardoned,
And it is in dying that we are
Born to Eternal Life.

And finally, we received a powerful prayer as part of our armor against Satan and all evil spirits, which we memorized, and today is prayed at the end of Catholic Masses by many churches:

Prayer of Saint Michael

Saint Michael, the Archangel, defend us in battle,
Be our protection against
The wickedness and snares of the devil,
May God rebuke him we humbly pray.
And do thou,
Oh prince of the heavenly Host,
By the power of God,
Cast into hell Satan and all the evil spirits,
Who wander through the world,
Seeking the ruin of souls.

Amen

We learned from the sisters that our lives as consecrated sisters are about helping those who need to find peace, need hope, need to learn how to be forgiven, need the light of Christ within them, need to find a deeper spirituality, and need joy.

I was beginning to see why Jesus spoke to me increasingly over two years, called me early one morning with the gift of my mother being present, and opened every door that needed to be opened to allow me to proceed with this calling. He intended to use all of my experience as a mother and retired businesswoman, to help others in many ways. That is a joyful thought.

This journey was beginning to make sense.

We were taught that the "I" factor in us dies, and that we serve others, not ourselves. We become filled with God's love to help others. This is the life God wants for us, translated by Jesus for us, on behalf of God.

Another day of doubting came. Satan loves it when we doubt what God asks us to do. This time, I felt as though no one in my community understood me. I did not seem to get along well with anyone at that particular time, *although this was not true most of the time.* Everyone has days like this. I was unhappy that day for reasons I do not even remember.

I recorded the date because what I heard during my prayer with Jesus made it an important day. It was January 12, 2013. *Jesus said, "I understand you."* He said this repeatedly, and it is precisely what I needed to hear. He has a way of interceding just when we need it. This was God's grace for me. And now I realize that it is not just me he understands; he understands all of you who are reading this book. No matter how difficult or complicated you think your life is, Jesus is walking with you AND understands you in ways no one else could.

I remembered that I, too, am a divine creation of God and worthy of his love, and love from others. I needed to remind myself that I am a unique design with my own individual personality, as is every person in this world. *And sometimes, all these unique individuals with their distinctive characteristics clash over ideas. That is okay because it is our differences that make us an interesting society. We can also learn from one another as we share our thoughts and feelings.*

After part of our formation was completed in Texas, the other candidate and I reported to the formation house, Casa

Corazon de Maria, in Tijuana, Mexico, to continue with the rest of our formation.

We continued with our daily regimen of prayer, Mass, serving the poor, chores, and visiting inmates in the Tijuana Federal Penitentiary. At our gated house, we received the poor, giving them peanut butter and jelly sandwiches, and water. They rang the doorbell at the gate that rang inside of our formation house.

One of us would scurry to the gate to inquire about their needs. We helped them as best we could. Even those of us who did not know Spanish somehow always found a way to communicate. A handshake and smile help when there is a communication barrier.

Tijuana has many people living in poverty without food, water, lodging, and medical care. Many have mental illness and do not receive the care they need, much like the approximate 60% who are incarcerated in United States prisons.[69]

Many of the people we serve in Tijuana are transients. They are people who are trying to enter into, or have been deported from, the United States. Of course, most of the time if they are deported, they do not receive travel funds to return home. People who have traveled from areas south of Mexico, and end up in Tijuana, need assistance anywhere they can find it. Many have come to our mission houses there, and they are fed.

We served in the Tijuana prison, visiting men and women. When we approached the prison with our rolling carts, there were guards with all-black attire, masks, machine guns, heavy boots, and radios. They know us very well and they let us in when it is safe.

---

[69] American Psychological Association feature article, *Incarceration Nation*, October 2014, Vol 45, No. 9.

We sign in, and we are screened for entry. They inspect everything we take in. Next, we go into a closed room where a female guard checks our pockets. We receive stamps with ink on our wrists.

We wait to walk through one gated entry to go to the storage room, "*bodega*" in Spanish, which has many of the supplies we need to give to the inmates. It is adjacent to Mother Antonia's cell. The Crucifix, twin bed, and the bathroom with shower and toilet are still the same as when she lived there.

After we load our carts with items purchased with donations, we walk through at least three gated entryways to arrive at the "paseo" (walk in Spanish), where we work for that day.

A sister and I served 150 men in two hours. The cells were approximately ten by fifteen feet in size, holding as many as twenty men in one cell, with one shower and toilet.

The inmates did not receive soap, toothbrushes, toothpaste, toilet paper, reading materials, Rosaries, candy, underclothing, and blankets, unless we brought it to them.

As a side note, it occurred to me while I was writing this book, during the beginning of the COVID-19 pandemic, that many people who are not incarcerated, but sheltering in place, unexpectedly experienced a glimpse of what it is like to be incarcerated. We temporarily lost many freedoms, like that of prisoners. We were confined to our homes.

The men were so appreciative that we would even care to visit them. They called us "Mama" in honor of Mother Antonia. Or they would call us "Hermana," which is Spanish for sister.

I especially remember that incarcerated U.S. citizens needed our help to contact family members because their families did not know they were in the Tijuana prison. Their phones are confiscated at the time of the arrest. We contacted their family members, asking them to get in touch with the Mexican U.S. Consulate to work on getting them extradited to the United States, if possible. We also contacted families of incarcerated Mexicans when they asked us to, to let their families know they were in the Tijuana prison.

Another memory was serving in the area of the prison where men had just been arrested the night before. Many of them were bruised and bloodied. We would see injuries such as swollen eyes and broken bones. They were filthy and their clothing was torn.

Next to these cells was an area called "Protection." This is where convicted police officers were held. It is the worst part of the prison I saw personally. More than twenty men were crammed into each of the two small cells. It was very dark, with very little light coming from a couple small windows.

As I prayed with them, I could see out of the corner of my eye, a line of roaches on the wall next to me, marching into the cells, towards the men. Everywhere I looked was unsanitary. The cell bars, clothing, the men—all were dirty. I am sure lice must have been present too.

We have minimal time in this area and have to hurriedly distribute the items we brought for the men in Protection. The reason for the urgency is that they were at high risk to be killed by other prisoners.

"Cell Block 6" has been known as the most dangerous area of the prison. In the past we were not allowed to go there, for our protection, and by the warden's orders. At one time, an inmate beheaded another inmate. Many of these inmates are criminals with repeated heinous crimes. At one time sisters could only go into this area on Ash Wednesday, to help distribute ashes to those who wanted them.

There is no heating or air conditioning of any kind in this prison. Blankets are especially crucial in the winter because otherwise, men sleep on concrete floors. They also double up on twin-size bunk beds, and under the bunk beds. There are usually two sets of three-tiered bunk beds in each cell. With twenty men to a cell, and not enough bunk beds, one can see the importance of blankets in the winter.

We also spent time helping at Casa Campos de San Miguel, serving drinks and sandwiches to the poor. This is a safe place for women leaving prison and for women visiting family in the Tijuana prison. It is a place for women and children who come to Tijuana for the treatment of cancer. Many transients come to this house to receive food and drink.

There is a beautiful chapel in the courtyard, a place where anyone who lives there can pray. A couple of our sisters, Sister Aisha and Sister Lourdes, facilitate the needs of the people who come to the mission house.

At Casa Corazon de Maria, Sister Nelida and Sister Anne Marie give food and drink to people at the gate. At Casa Corazon de Jesus, Sister Ann Gertrude and Sister Carmen, serve those who are in need at the gate as well. Sister Viola resides at our United States location in San Diego, and comes over the border to visit with those in prison who prepare to go before the courts (Juzgados in Spanish).

We have vowed sisters all over the United States, retired and active, who work in various ministries of mercy, including prison ministry,[70] teaching, hospital chaplaincy, St. Vincent de Paul Society conference and council-level work, immigration, homebound ministry, and pastoral duties, for example.

---

[70] This includes pen pal, visiting death row inmates; also, online prison ministry faith formation and re-entry.

As time allows, the sisters have visited Las Memorias on the edge of Tijuana, a hospice/drug rehabilitation facility for people with HIV, started by Tony Granillo. We visited with very sick patients, some who were actively dying. I only visited this place a couple times, due to our schedule. Tony was formerly incarcerated at the Tijuana Federal Penitentiary, where he met Mother Antonia. Volunteers from the medical profession traveled from the United States to help care for those who live there.

At the end of each day of ministries, we enjoyed our community time together, praying, eating a meal together, sharing our stories, listening, and supporting one another. I hoped to spend time with Mother Antonia in my first year of meeting her, which was in March 2013.

It was my turn to make dinner for the house. It was Friday during Lent, no meat, and I baked fish. Mother heard about the fish and she asked for some. I was happy to make sure she received the fish.

I walked across the street to Casa Corazon de Jesus, where mother lived. She was on the phone with one of her grown children singing "When Irish Eyes Are Smiling" because it was Saint Patrick's Day. She was Irish, and so am I. I told her that our mother used to sing that song to us. I was so surprised! She then sang it to me! That was an extraordinary moment I will always treasure.

That day I asked a sister to take our picture together as this was my first meeting with mother. We both happened to be wearing black-and-white aprons! I asked her to autograph my copy of *The Prison Angel*, her biography, and she said she would be happy to sign it.

With Mother Antonia on St. Patrick's Day
in Casa Corazon de Jesus - 2013

The Feast Day of the Annunciation arrived, March 25, 2013. This is the day first vows of new sisters are made, and a renewal of vows for the existing sisters. I should have made my first vows that day, but I could not because I did not have an annulment. My priest, Father Brian, advised it was necessary to have a clear path to the cross before I could make my first vows.

At that time, my ex-husband was alive, and although I was divorced and never remarried, *not* having an annulment was an encumbrance to making my first vows. I would have to wait. I waited for what seemed to be an eternity.

I returned to where I began formation, Lockhart, Texas, while I waited for the annulment. I continued working in the Saint Vincent de Paul Society ministry, prison ministry, and as a sacristan and lector, as well as doing household chores and errands.

Several months later, I was permitted by the formation house mother, Sister Lillian, to return to my home to prepare my house for sale. The mortgage payment was draining my savings and I knew that after I received the annulment, I would make my vows and return to Georgia. I thought I would receive the annulment at any time.

I invited Sister to accompany me on the drive back to my home. She had a good friend there she wanted to visit, *the same woman* who sat next to me at the retreat, who said I should talk to a friend of hers in Texas (Sister Lillian).

We began our trip Sunday after morning Mass and stopped in Arkansas for lunch. We both like Chick-Fil-A, so I pulled into the parking lot. Neither of us remembered it was Sunday and the restaurant was closed. We also did not notice there were no cars in the parking lot because we were so busy talking!

As I closed my car door and walked toward the restaurant, I heard Sister laughing. I walked around the back of the car toward her to see what was so funny. Her scapular, which is the piece we wear over the dress, was lifted up by the wind and caught in the car door on the passenger side of the car. The door would not open. The scapular material somehow caused the door to jam. We worked on getting the door open. We pushed and pulled the material with a writing pen. Sister thought she would cut the scapular, then decided to simply pull it over her head, and tossed it into the car. The scapular was still stuck in the door jam. The door would not open, no matter what we tried to do. She suggested that I get inside the car and try to kick the door open from the inside. That did not work.

All this time, we did not notice there were quite a few patrons at the Huddle House next door, watching us. They were probably thinking, "What are those crazy nuns doing?" No one came to help us either, by the way.

Sister thought we might call a local mechanic to help us. I reminded her it was Sunday and that no one would help us on Sunday.

Then I said, "Sister, we have not prayed yet." So, we prayed. She prayed her prayer, and I prayed mine. I said, "Jesus, please release her scapular!" God heard both of our prayers, I'm sure.

We waited patiently after this. We let go. What did God do?

We chatted for a little while, standing next to the car, but not leaning against it, and then something told me to look down at the car door. *Suddenly, the door was ajar by one-half inch, barely noticeable.* How could it be that the door was open? We had not been able to open it. We surrendered the problem to God. He took over.

The moral of the story is that as we attempt to solve problems in our daily lives, we need to pray before we do the work, asking for help. We need to pray while we are doing the work, and if we still need help, surrender the rest to God.

Some say it this way—do your best and give God the rest. *After the problem is resolved, pray to give thanks to God for whatever the outcome is.* As prayerful Christians, we pray before, during, and after communicating with God all along the way.

My thoughts during this event were that if we did not get the passenger door open, I was going to have to drive "Ms. Daisy" (Sister Lillian) with her in the back seat, all the way to my home! I am sure sister did not want to be chauffeured during the entire trip either!

This was another unexplained mystical event that I could not explain reasonably or logically. God took care of this, answering our prayers, and because they were in accordance with his will for us. *That is the only logical explanation.*

Three more events occurred during this time. The first happened at my home. The last two incidents took place in Lockhart, Texas. All three were direct attacks by Satan to scare me away from my calling from Jesus. After each attack, I sought a special blessing from the local priest, Father Brian at my home parish, and Father Alberto of the parish in Texas, and spent additional time in adoration of the Blessed Sacrament.

Both priests reassured me this is normal for anyone answering a calling. Satan does not want us to be successful, because if we are, and we become consecrated sisters, he knows we will bring souls to Christ.

If you, the reader, doubt if these events occurred, please research the lives of Saints Padre Pio, Teresa of Avila, Ignatius of Loyola, Catherine of Siena, Francis of Assisi, and Benedict, for example. Dr. Paul Thigpen provides short summaries of demonic attacks against these saints in his *Manual of Spiritual Warfare*.[71]

Spiritual warfare is real. It is no joke. It is part of the journey of becoming a priest, deacon, brother, or sister, because of what we will do for God once we have completed formation, and are either ordained or consecrated.

The first attack happened on June 7, 2013. Of course, I recorded these. This was on the Solemnity of the Sacred Heart of Jesus, at 2:45 a.m. I will just share here that the best defense against this is to stay "armored up." This means to stay in daily prayer, especially praying the Rosary, receiving the Eucharist at Mass, for example, and removing evil from your life, of course. Strive to become more holy every day.

Getting back to purging my personal items to prepare my home for sale - It took me three months to go through every

---

[71] Paul Thigpen, *Manual for Spiritual Warfare* (Charlotte, North Carolina: Tan Books, 2015).

item I owned in the house to decide what items I would donate to the church, and to charities. All of my business suits, shoes, accessories, recreation equipment, knick-knacks, kitchen items, and gardening equipment were donated.

What was most difficult to donate was a huge Ficus plant I grew from a clipping of my mother's plant thirty-five years ago, when my first two sons, Chris and Joey, were five and three years old. It was too big to ask a family member to take care of for me, but I had to find a home for it because I had to sell the house. I donated it to my church. Finally, everything leftover from the purging process was going into storage in Georgia, while I was in formation.

My sons, friends, and a neighbor helped to move my remaining belongings into a storage unit. I still cannot believe it all fit into one unit, except for two pieces of furniture I no longer needed.

Then I returned to Lockhart, Texas, to work in ministries while I waited for the annulment. I was attacked by Satan two more times. Still, before they would happen, I experienced the Holy Spirit in a significant way.

On August 16, 2013, three priests held a charismatic Mass and healing service at Santa Cruz Catholic Church in Buda, Texas. It was at this Mass that I fell for the first time, resting in the Holy Spirit of God. A new priest who had never anointed a person with blessed oil during a healing service, barely touched my forehead, and I immediately collapsed to the floor. The extremities of my fingers and toes were twitching. The twitching hasn't happened again since this first time.[72] Usually, after I collapse, I am still, and cannot move at first. After some time, I can move again, and someone helps me to stand up. It is a unique spiritual event

---

[72] I have rested in the spirit seven times during charismatic Catholic services.

every time, a personal moment in time, with the Holy Spirit of God.

I experienced two more attacks, one on September 13, 2013, and another on September 30, 2013. After each attack, I met with the Lockhart priest, Father Alberto, to share the details of what happened. Each time, after I received his blessing, he reassured me this was normal for someone who says yes to the calling. It is spiritual warfare.

I asked Father what he does when this kind of thing happens to him. He said that sometimes he would hear things rattling in his rectory, and he knows it is just Satan trying to scare him again. I said, "What do you do?" He said as he props his chin against the palm of his hand, that he says to Satan, "Oh, it's you again." He is calm in his delivery of this message to Satan, brushing him off, as his attacks are expected and ineffective. This helped me a great deal.

These attacks were part of my formation journey. They were unsettling to me. Yet, I overcame them, because I did not lose my focus of the calling. *I could not let fear deter me. Throughout the Bible, we are told not to be afraid.*[73]

Laughter is an effective way of deterring evil. It removes fear and sadness, and brings joy to our hearts. Haven't we noticed those wonderful comical people who are great to have around to crack a [clean] joke, just when we need it? My brother, Bobby, is one of those folks. Just like our Dad, who was always telling good jokes.

What we need to realize is that attacks can happen, but what is more important is knowing how to armor ourselves in battle against Satan and all his evil spirits. *Stay prayed up. Pray unceasingly. Receive the Sacraments. Bless yourself with Holy Water. Be vigilant, staying faithful to the Gospels of Jesus.*

---

[73] A few Biblical references: Gen. 15:1, Ex. 14:13, Josh. 1:9, and Mt. 1:20.

Be at peace. And these are just a few ways of armoring ourselves in battle against Satan.

The most important thing I learned while in formation was true humility. Before entering formation, I could be defensive and self-centered at times. In formation, we learn that life is not about us; it is about everyone else, especially those who are the least of our brothers and sisters. I had to learn how to humble myself in all situations, recognizing that it is not always necessary to defend my position on a disagreement, or to ensure that my desires are always met, for example.

I learned this new perspective of life through the acts of kindness of consecrated sisters.

Questions for the reader to contemplate: Does it sound as though formation is challenging? Do I believe that if Jesus calls me to serve, God will give me the grace to get through it? Knowing that God provides, can I see myself striving to embrace changes? Despite evil attacks that may occur, do I trust that I will learn how to armor myself, and that God will pull me through?

CHAPTER 8
ABANDONMENT OF SELF THROUGH PRAYER

A bandonment of self is dying to self.

Blaise Pascal, the seventeenth-century philosopher said, "All of human evil comes from a single cause, man's inability to sit still in a room."[74]

At the beginning of the 2020 pandemic in the United States, people were ordered to stay home to help stop the spread of the highly contagious COVID-19 virus. For some, this was welcome, much-needed downtime to rest. For others who live with family members, this time may or may not have been fruitful; instead, it may have been stressful if the family was prone to conflict anyway. We pray for those families who continue to experience domestic violence even more so because the children and parents were home 24/7. Hopefully the parents were able to find some level of peace by creating innovative ways for their family members to interact peacefully.

Philosopher Blaise Pascal refers to sitting quietly in a room alone. My favorite scripture is Psalm 46:10, "Be still

---

[74] Blaise Pascal, *Pensées*, trans. Roger Ariew (Indianapolis, Indiana: Hacket Publishing Company, 2004), 38.

and know that I am God." Why my favorite? Because without sitting in the silence, we cannot come to know who God is.

I agree with Pascal, because if we talked (prayed) with God first, asking him for help, before we approach humanity's problems, we would know what God wants us to do. Instead, we tend to execute our plans without God.

Sitting silently is the first step to abandoning ourselves. Why is this important? The hardest part of the battle to improving oneself is when we finally muster the courage to commit to change. Work is necessary on our part to become more holy in the eyes of the Lord. Then we continuously strive to become more holy, even after a person is ordained or consecrated.

As a sister once told me, "Light a candle, show up, and shut up." I now share this with others who want to know how to change; instead, I say, "Light a candle, show up, and be quiet." Our foundress, Mother Antonia, stressed to us to speak with love and kindness, to be careful with our words.

This advice means, stop talking so much, be quiet, and be open to hearing what God may want to tell you. This is how a person develops a friendship with Jesus, welcoming him into your heart.

God waits for you. He waits for you to be still and to be quiet, so he can speak to you. Be patient to hear him. It takes time. Remove distractions.

Once we take these first steps—along with learning to purge our old baggage from ourselves, emptying ourselves of the old sins and past hurts, receiving and giving forgiveness—we can then prepare to receive the Holy Spirit of God. He wants us to know his unconditional love for us.

When I experienced my Cursillo[75] weekend experience, we took our old baggage (the past) to a burning fire pit at night, as we prayed. We received the following beautiful piece that suggests we leave our past sins, sorrows, burdens, afflictions, brokenness, at the foot of the Cross of Jesus. We surrendered all these things to God, once and for all:

Burn it by the Cross[76]

If you have a secret sorrow,
a burden or a loss,
An aching need for healing...

Burn it by the Cross

If worries steal your sleep
and make you turn and toss,
If your heart is feeling heavy...

Burn it by the Cross

Every obstacle to faith
or doubt you come across,
Every prayer unanswered...

Burn it by the Cross

For Christ has borne
our brokenness
and dearly paid the cost
To turn our trials to triumph...

Burn it by the Cross

The work that is involved in changing ourselves willingly, prepares us to become a better version of ourselves. It is

---

[75] To learn more, visit *www.natl-cursillo.org*.
[76] A paraphrase of the "Hang It on the Cross" prayer card by Lisa O. Engelhardt. (St. Meinrad, Indiana: Abbey Press, 2001).

unhealthy to continue to carry burdens. *Who are we saving our burdens for?* And as Father Brian at my home parish said during his homily, "Why do we continue to pick the scab and allow ourselves to bleed?"

Some people continue to carry their burdens as though they are badges of honor, speaking of them often. Do we simply not know how to rid ourselves of these burdens? Do we trust God to take them away, if we try to release them to him?

Once we abandon those things within us that are not of God, and are free of them, we are then able to be filled with good things from the Holy Spirit of God. We learn the values and virtues of Jesus Christ in the Bible. Then we apply the way, the truth, and the life of Jesus to our own lives, making changes within us, where changes are needed.

We become someone new, no longer the same person we were. The title of the first chapter of this book reminds us of this - *You Are Who You Aren't*. We commit to the changes we need to make and welcome Jesus. We are renewed in Christ. As it is stated in the book of Romans, "Do not be conformed to this world but be transformed by the renewal of your mind, that you may prove what the will of God is, what is good and acceptable and perfect" (Rom. 12:2).

Once I had a re-occurring dream for some time every night. I believed I saw Jesus in these dreams, but his face was always unrecognizable. I knew it was him though. These were dreams, not nightmares. I did not understand the dreams. In the dreams, people were brought to Jesus continually so that he could help them. Then Sister Lillian, during my come-and-see visit in September, 2011, gave me a prayer card about abandoning self.

Prayer of Abandonment[77]

Father,
I abandon myself into your hands;
do with me what you will.
Whatever you may do, I thank you;
I am ready for all, I accept all.

Let only your will be done in me,
and in all your creatures.
I wish no more than this, Oh Lord.

Into your hands I commend my soul;
I offer it to you
with all the love of my heart,
for I love you, Lord,
and so need to give myself,
to surrender myself into your hands,
without reserve,
and with boundless confidence,
for you are my Father. Amen.

by Charles de Foucauld

I cried when she gave me this prayer card, because it was at this same time of having these unexplainable dreams, that she gave it to me. On the reverse side is a picture of Jesus Christ, labeled "The Face of Christ." It seemed to somehow satisfy my curiosity of why Jesus did not have a face in my dreams.

I finally realized the importance of this faceless Christ in my dream, recognizing that God will always bring me another person. The face always changes, but the need remains. Those

---

[77] Republished recently in *Charles de Foucauld: Writings, Modern Spiritual Masters,* Robert Ellsberg ed. (Maryknoll, NY: Orbis, 1999), 104.

of us who minister to others believe we see Christ in everyone, regardless of what baggage they may carry. For some, it is harder to see Christ, but he is most definitely there.

When a baby is created, God creates a soul for this divine creation. The Catholic Catechism states that "The Church teaches that every spiritual soul is created immediately by God—it is not 'produced' by the parents—and also that it is immortal: it does not perish when it separates from the body at death, and it will be reunited with the body at the final Resurrection."[78]

Recognizing this truth of the existence of the soul, goes to the very basis of why the dignity of life must be respected, whether it is an unborn child, an unused embryo during in vitro fertilization, assisted suicide, or taking a life early through the imposition of the death penalty.

The essence of the abandonment prayer is that we wish to accept whatever God's Will is for us, and to let go of our own will. I consistently ask him to do with me what he wants, to use me as his vessel to help others.

Have you wondered how some folks are filled with endless joy, regardless of what happens in their lives? How did they become this way? What are they doing to receive the light they carry? And where did that light come from?

Once we make the necessary changes to find peace within ourselves, we eventually come to know the fullness of the light of Jesus Christ. We carry that light to others in our daily interactions. *We let go of those things in life that drag us down into the pit of despair.* After all, these things are what entertain the evil one the most. He sees us continually punishing ourselves over past sins, hurt, and pain, unless we stop this habit of self-punishment.

---

[78] CCC 366

When people say, "I can see a light around her," they see the light of Jesus in her, because she is living the way, the truth, and the life of Jesus. Joy and peace are eventually experienced by applying the values and virtues of Jesus found in the New Testament of the Bible. We strive to follow him.

Forming oneself is a daily *and* life-long process. Like any process, forming oneself cannot happen overnight, and involves many changes. This is true even after we make our first vows as consecrated sisters, we continue to form ourselves, to strive to become better versions of ourselves.

Saint John Eudes, the patron saint of our association of sisters, wrote a beautiful letter to a contemporary of his, Mother Patin. His words are very insightful on the work involved in annihilating ourselves at the feet of Jesus:

"Therefore, give yourself to him, my dearest Mother, that you may suffer with him in that condition and in that spirit, as much as he desires. Try to do three things:

1) Try not to become disheartened, guarding well against it. Surrender to divine virtue and strength that they may sustain you.

2) Accept this state of death and annihilation, saying with the Son of God: 'Father, into your hands I commend my spirit' (Lk. 23:46).

3) Abandon yourself entirely to the most holy will of God, repeating with Our Lord: 'Not my will but yours be done' (Lk. 22:42)."[79]

Catholic congregations have always experienced challenges in how to form their candidates. Eudist theologian, Steven Marshall, who works with the Congregation of Jesus and Mary, explained in an email to me:

---

[79] Bishop Clément Guillon, *In All Things, The Will of God*, trans. Louis Levesque (Solana Beach, California: Eudist Press, 2019).

She [Mother Patin] was a Sister of the Visitation and somewhat of a specialist in training women to live community life. When SJE [Saint John Eudes] first founded OLC [the Sisters of Our Lady of Charity], she agreed to live with the new community for what ended up being a couple decades, serving as novice mistress and superior (remaining a Visitation sister both during and after).[80]

In the previous chapter, I discussed formation in general, with humility being the most challenging virtue for me personally. The virtue of obedience was new to me too because I had been a manager and was used to being in charge. In formation, I was not used to simply obeying authority, especially when I thought I had a better solution.

We will never be perfect in this earthly life, but we can strive to become more holy.

I had to learn to let go of my ego and worldly experience, unless I was asked what I thought. This was necessary because the journey of a sister is not about all the things we accomplished in our former lives. Generally, it is not useful in the life of a sister, although at times our past skills, talents, and abilities, come in handy.

Learning to be obedient also taught me to have more patience. I still struggle with these things even today, because my past work experiences have been part of me for so many years.

We begin to abandon the person we are, in order to become an improved, renewed version of ourselves. We begin to use the teachings of Jesus to apply to daily situations.

---

[80] The Sisters of Our Lady of Charity, an order of sisters founded by Saint John Eudes in 1641.

Gradually, we become better versions of ourselves. The old person does not go away completely; however, we begin to see things differently and in a positive light. We begin to mature in our faith along the way. Like any temptation, the tendency to return to old behavior can still happen, and to refuse this old behavior takes commitment and persistence.

After we commit to turning to God by sitting in the silence, we open ourselves to receive him, to listen to him. During one of the retreats I attended, before I started formation, we were given this prayer:

Now
Oh Lord,
calm me into a quietness
that heals
and listens,
and molds my longings
and passions,
my wounds
and wonderings
into a more holy
and human
shape.[81]

by Ted Loder

Capuchin Father Emiliano Antenucci presented an image of Our Lady of Silence to Pope Francis at the Vatican on March 22, 2019. Father Antenucci said that silence "…is the womb where words that are true are born."[82] This image

---

[81] Ted Loder, *Guerillas of Grace: Prayers for the Battle* (Minneapolis: Augsburg Books, 2005), 27.

[82] Carol Glatz "Spirituality of silence is a journey toward God, the priest says," *The Georgia Bulletin*, August 8, 2019, *www.georgiabulletin.org/news/2019/08/spirituality-of-silence-is-a-journey-toward-god-priest-says.*

of Our Blessed Mother suggests we stay in the silence, an essential part of our Christian existence.

God already knows where we are and what we are doing. He waits patiently for us day after day. Once we remove distractions, we can turn to him to sit in the silence with him.

We then finally realize we have ignored God. When I realized this, I felt sad and remorseful. I was then motivated to abandon more of my old self to become who he was waiting for me to become.

God, in his mercy, forgives us, and we begin again. We have the opportunity to become renewed in Christ, to carry the light of Christ to others, to do his will, not our will.

Other forms of abandonment are emptying our closets, dressers, kitchen cabinets, and storage. We can also make more drastic changes depending upon our journeys. Choosing to belong to an association of sisters can result in no longer wearing cosmetics, cutting off hair, and wearing the habit and veil. And these things are liberating. No more curling irons, makeup or hair dryers! Abandon our old ways of living to make way for what God has prepared for us. And they are things we do not need to help us serve the least of our brothers and sisters.

We are left with inner peace.

Questions for the reader to contemplate: What baggage do I continue to carry that I need to get rid of? What drastic changes am I willing to make, to answer the calling to serve those who suffer?

CHAPTER 9
COMMITMENTS AS A MOTHER, GRANDMOTHER, AND SISTER

One of the questions I am most frequently asked is, "What do your children think about this?" They are referring to being a Catholic sister. I say, "Some of them are still scratching their heads about this, but I think that by now they know I am serious about this life change." It is the same answer when someone asks me what my siblings think.

I believe this is one of the reasons Jesus told me to "write the book," to share the journey with my family. There were more details than I could have ever relayed to all of my family members about these drastic changes.

My husband and I raised three sons. They are parents now. Their lovely wives and children are my family. I do not get to see them very often. I pray for them daily. Because I love all of them so much, I pray they will always have what they need, including strength, courage, patience, perseverance, good health, faith, and wisdom.

The bond between a parent and the child is never broken. It can become strained, distant, or estranged at its worst; however, the bond is eternal. This is our faith as Catholics, and this is what

I personally believe. We have hope to be reunited with all of those we love after we physically die.

Our lives here are extremely short in comparison to the infinity of eternal life with God. This is why it is wise to strive to become as holy as we can in this life, and *not* offend (sin against) God. We also need to prepare for the transition to eternal life in heaven by reconciling our sins with him, asking for forgiveness.

Family Photo – Dad, Mom, Bobby, Joey, Chris – 1988

Our three sons – Chris, Bobby,
Joey – 1989

Our Family - At Grandma and Grandpa McDonald's house for a
family reunion -1992
Mom, Chris, Bobby, Joey, and Dad

As Catholics, we believe we will enter purgatory first, then God willing, heaven. As the Catechism states, "All who die in God's grace and friendship, but still imperfectly purified, are indeed assured of their eternal salvation; but after death, they undergo purification, to achieve the holiness necessary to enter the joy of heaven."[83]

A frequent comment I make when talking about the subject of death to others is, "I don't know about you, but I do not want my final story to end six feet under!" I look forward to being reunited with all of my family members in heaven. I cannot wait to be with my mother, father, sister, and even my ex-husband again. I miss them, yet I know they are watching over our family.

Mother Antonia Brenner, our foundress of the Eudist Servants of the Eleventh Hour, gave birth to eight children.

---

[83] CCC 1030

She raised seven children; one child died at childbirth. She will always be their mother. From heaven, she watches over them.

At fifty years old, she received a calling from Jesus she could not say no to, serving her spiritually-adopted sons and daughters in the Tijuana Federal Penitentiary. She became their spiritual mother and greatly loved them.

Our Blessed Mother Mary gave birth to salvation, with the birth of Jesus. Her bond with him will continue forever. She is with him in heaven, along with her husband, Joseph. They have been reunited as the Holy Family and they, too, watch over my family. I pray, asking the Holy Family to be with my sons and their families.

The parental commitment happens at the moment of conception and continues forever. These natural maternal and paternal bonds begin at conception. We only die physically; the soul, another component of every human being, and the family bonds, last into eternity.

My sons no longer needed my nurturing and care once they left the nest. They became completely independent. It would not have been psychologically healthy for me to sit around lamenting over the significant loss of my sons in their independence. This is the letting go process that is in everyone's best interest.

Letting go of my sons to release them to their wives and children, was heart-breaking, yet another normal event of raising a family. When they were children, I was their mother, their primary focus for many years. Now, I am not the primary focus, and that is okay. *This is normal and necessary for the well-being of everyone in the family.* These are easy words to type, but at times, challenging to live with.

Although I still yearn to be with my family, and this is natural, I am grateful knowing my sons have matured to the point of knowing their focus *must* primarily be on their own families now. It does not mean they no longer love me. They still love me, and I love them. And now I have more family members to love because their families have grown. They are all blessings from God. I am grateful to have every one of them in my life.

Having recognized that I was an empty nester, and my sons had their own lives, I followed my calling to become a consecrated sister. It was taking a long time. Other new candidates who began formation after me, were making their first vows. I was not. I continued to wait for the annulment on the advice of my home parish priest.

My formation was completed in March 2013. That summer, I was given permission to purge the personal belongings at my home. The house sold several months later. I was thankful because the mortgage was draining my savings, even though I was no longer living there.

Returning to Lockhart, Texas, I continued to work in ministries of mercy, while I waited for the annulment. This time of my life is filled with so many stories.

The Saint Vincent de Paul Society vice president of our conference, Hortencia, continued to mentor me in serving the poor, using Catholic Church donations. I had phone duty every day for a week at a time, taking calls from people who were in critical need. This was how our conference facilitated intake calls from the public.

Hortencia gave me invaluable lessons of serving those who suffer, teaching me how we grow spiritually, as a Vincentian, through service to our brothers and sisters, and seeing the "suffering Christ" in them. Today I draw upon those lessons to teach other Vincentians, as the St. Vincent de Paul Society-Georgia Council Spiritual Advisor. I have lead retreats, developed formation material, and helped

Vincentians learn the primary focus of being a Vincentian, which is to grow spiritually.

We visited homes to assess a family's needs and bring them groceries from the food pantry. I was living in a small Texas town where there were few jobs, and those who were able to work still received an exceptionally low income. There never seemed to be enough money to help everyone. My heart broke for so many of them, because it seemed our help was so little compared to everything they needed.

Having been a mother with a family budget, I sometimes made budget recommendations to Saint Vincent de Paul Society clients who were in need. God was using my gifts.

One afternoon, a man walked into the parish office off the street to ask for help. He was brought to our Saint Vincent de Paul Society office to speak with another Vincentian and me. Recently released from prison, he somehow found his way to the church. He did not have any money or form of payment of any kind. He needed everything, because he had nothing but the clothes on his back. We told him we would help him.

Laughing, I still remember my fellow Vincentian and friend, Hortencia, sharing with me she was going to go into her husband's closet to give this man some of his clothes. She said she did not think her husband would even miss them! She brought them back to the office from her house and had with her a well-made button-down long sleeve shirt and a nice pair of jeans.

I, on the other hand, had the responsibility of going to the Dollar General store to buy him undergarments, socks, and other personal items. I did not mind because I used to buy the same things for my sons when they were growing up. Still, I laughed in the store, standing in front of a shelf of men's boxers and briefs, thinking to myself, "What in the world am I doing buying undergarments for a man, a stranger I do not even know? I don't even know which he prefers, boxers or briefs!" Had I not had the experience of buying undergarments for the opposite gender, I am not sure my mission would have been successful.

Another time, actually my first home visit with Hortencia, we arrived literally at a little old shack on the outskirts of town. A chihuahua greeted us, who seemed fierce, but was harmless. Old, heavily used, children's toys were strewn about in the fenced front yard. We went to the front door and knocked. The mother invited us in. The place was one room that had one bed, television, and a fan. There was no air conditioning. It was sweltering hot in Texas. Several children ran around the room. Another woman was lying on the bed.

There was no place to sit except on the edge of the bed. We sat there with the mother, who had contacted us on the phone. Hortencia conducted the home visit, while I observed and listened. She was mentoring me. *At the end of the visit, I asked the women what they would like us to pray for. The other woman began to cry. I have seen repeatedly that just asking someone how we can pray for them can be a very emotional experience. This offer of prayer allows them to both know and feel that someone cares about them.* We consoled her, not knowing what the issue was. She was not willing to share this with us. She did not have to share with us. We just wanted her to know that we were present and would lend a listening ear if she needed it. We reassured her, then we prayed together. We were able to help the family, informing them of what we could do. Then we left.

I share these stories to highlight what Mother Antonia Brenner, our foundress, demonstrated for us as well. *She remained a mother and grandmother even after she became a consecrated sister.* She lived in a prison cell for over thirty years, never committed a crime, and performed her ministries. She never stopped being a mother to her own biological children along the way of her journey.

In our association of sisters, God uses our experience as mothers, grandmothers, and retirees, to help others in need. It is our purpose at this stage of our lives as sisters. We bring our nurturing and consoling dispositions, education, faith, as well as the wisdom we gained over the years, to guide those whom God sends to us to help.

As our children age and become independent, we are not needed as much anymore by our families. We do not receive as many phone calls and visits from them because they have their own lives to live with their spouses and children. And that is normal and okay.

We are empty-nesters who have a lot to offer. While we may be called by God late-in-life to serve others, this does not mean we forget our families.

One of the requirements of being accepted into the Eudist Servants association is that we cannot have dependents to care for in our homes. All three of my sons are financially self-sufficient adults. No one is living with me or depends on me.

The Feast Day of the Holy Family in the Catholic Church celebrates the family of Jesus, Mary, and Joseph, and is focused on the importance of the family. We teach, nurture, console, lead, and love our children through their early years of life. We give them the necessary foundations in areas we believe are essential.

Back in our day as young parents, these foundations were hygiene, manners, school studies, responsibilities, Boy Scouts, and the Catholic faith.

Suddenly, they are grown young men, ready to leave the nest to begin their own lives. And we are not always prepared for this if we are mothers of sons. It is the same, I understand, for fathers of daughters. I cannot say for sure, though, because I never had a daughter. I have granddaughters, and it may become difficult for my sons to let go of them later when these girls leave the nest.

At some point, we must let go of our children. It is in their best interest, as well as ours.

"...his mother said to him, 'Son, why have you treated us so? Behold, your father and I have been looking for you anxiously. And he said to them, 'How is it that you sought me? Did you not know that I must be in my Father's house?'" (Lk. 2:48-49)

His parents see that Jesus has matured in his faith. They found him in the temple at twelve years old after having lost him for three days. He is coming into his own, so-to-speak, changing to evolve into a young man. He informed his parents that he needed to go about his business, following his Heavenly Father's orders to preach at the temple. And so, he did.

If our relationship with God is good, *and comes before anything else or anyone else*, there is a greater possibility of lasting harmony in our lives.

As humans we strive to know the higher power, who is God; and in a perfectly ordered world, an adult who is mature in their faith, will place God first, spouse second, and child last, considering the natural order of human relationships. *A spiritually mature human understands this order, yet still greatly loves their family.*

We *allow* God to be in charge. This is that arrogant statement again. When we allow God to be in charge, life is less of a struggle. I know this from experience. It was not until after the calling from Jesus that I took him to work with me. After this, the struggles I had, disappeared.

As a grandmother, I enjoy all the things other grandmothers do. I love to make homemade chocolate chip cookies with my grandchildren, buy toys, books, and clothes for them, chat, and play with them.

One of my grandsons, Dean, is three years old. He enjoys many things, including playing with cars, building things, playing outside, and doing activities with his parents. We enjoy sitting together while I read him books. We sing nursery songs together. We build towers with blocks, and then he enjoys immediately knocking them down—which is what three-year-old children do!

As the grandchildren get older, I enjoy other activities with them, such as drawing on the driveway with chalk, going for a walk, dancing in the kitchen, playing tic-tac-toe, card games, watching children's movies, cooking, and crafts. My grandchildren who are six and eight years old, Benicio and Luna, enjoy these types of activities.

My oldest grandchild, Olivia, is thirteen years old as of this writing. We enjoy eating cheeseburgers and watching the Andy Griffith show. She and I cook together, go shopping, play cards (double solitaire), and discuss the Christian faith. Sometimes she helps me with odd jobs around the house too, while sharing with her what I know about life.

All these things seem like a lot of activities, but the truth is, these special moments have been few and far between over the past thirteen years.

I am committed to the ministries God has called me to do. The grandchildren have school, sports, and activities with their own families. As long as we consider each other's schedules, we can coordinate events to spend time with each other every once in a while.

My daughters-in-law, Vanessa, Karen, and Robyn, are exceptionally gifted young women who dearly love their husbands and children. All of them are great mothers who are personally invested in the welfare of their family members. They work hard to ensure their families are well-cared for, and that their husbands and children know they are loved.

The little time I spend with my sons, daughters-in-law, and grandchildren, is precious to me. Yet, prison ministry is joyful and fulfilling, because I know I am doing what Jesus called me to do for him at this late stage in my life.

Balancing my two worlds of being a Catholic sister, and living my continual maternal life, almost always works.

My fifth grandchild, Dimara, arrived while this book was in draft and during the COVID-19 pandemic. She is another blessing from God.

A baby.

Questions for the reader to contemplate: If I am a middle-aged man or woman, called to be ordained or consecrated to serve the least of our brothers and sisters, and I am also a grandparent, will being a grandparent hinder my decision to say yes? If so, why?

CHAPTER 10
MAKING FIRST VOWS

I began my formation to become a sister in April 2012 and completed it in March 2013. Candidates who finish their formation, make their first vows[84] with the Eudist Servants of the Eleventh Hour on March 25th, which is the Solemnity of the Feast of the Annunciation. Our vows are temporary and renewed every year. What should have been my vows day of March 25, 2013, came and went. I did not make my vows because I did not have the annulment.

During the summer of 2013, my formation house mother gave me some time to purge my belongings at my home, to prepare it for sale, because I was no longer living there. Following this, I returned to Lockhart, Texas to work again in ministries.

In October 2013, my formation house mother gave me permission to relocate to Georgia, to begin working in ministries of mercy, while I waited for the annulment. The basis of this decision was because I knew after I made my first vows, I would live and work in Georgia.

I knew that once I completed formation, I was required to work in ministries of mercy wherever I would live. At this

---

[84] "First vows" in our association of the faithful means it is the first time we make our vows. In successive years, we renew our vows annually. Our procedure of making vows differs from that of a traditional order, which has more than one level of vows.

point, there was no reason to remain in Lockhart, since I had completed formation, and knew Georgia was where I would go after first vows.

Seven months later, on May 5, 2014, I received news that my ex-husband had passed away unexpectedly of congestive heart failure. This was an incredibly sad time for my sons and me. It was heart-wrenching, because it was only in his last couple of years of life that he and I began to have amicable discussions. Like all couples, we had our issues. And now he was gone.

God decided it was his time. None of us were ready for that. He was only sixty years old, taken from this life much too soon.

I was distraught when I received the news of his passing, and had a high stress level for some time after this. Initially, I felt cheated by God, upset with him about this. I had been married twenty-three years to this man, the father of my children, and finally had a mature friendship with him. We both needed to improve our marital relationship skills before we were divorced, and this process had finally begun some number of years after the divorce. Before he died, we forgave each another for past offenses. The wounds had begun to heal.

It took me awhile to get past this with God. I finally realized once again, God is in control, not me, so I did not need to spend another second being frustrated about this.

Soon after he passed, when I was at home alone, I entered the kitchen to find sunlight streaming into the kitchen that landed perfectly, and only, on him, in the last family photo taken with him in it. At that moment, I believed he was already in heaven. I knew this was true, there was no question in my mind, even though there was no way for me to prove this.

On July 25, 2014, I was in Eucharistic Adoration at the church. My rheumatoid arthritis and fibromyalgia had returned. Flaring from these diseases came back pretty severely due to the high stress I endured after the passing of my ex-husband, and witnessing the pain my sons were quietly enduring. I was prescribed potent medicines for the arthritis and fibromyalgia.

I had the usual symptoms I had before, but this time it was very short-lived, because I knew from previous experience how to control and eliminate the stress that caused it. Both diseases went back into remission, medicine was no longer needed after six months, and I have not flared since then.

This is the power of prayer, regaining calm, and inner peace.

Before the diseases went into remission, and while I was in Eucharistic Adoration, in prayer, I was questioning why I was suffering again with these diseases. Jesus told me, "I just want you to agonize with me for a while." My thoughts at that time were that he wants me to spend more time with him in prayer. And so, I did.

On a more recent occasion of being in pain from some other affliction, when I was talking with my spiritual director, Father Wise, he said, *"Please offer a portion of your cross for me as I pray for you."* These were comforting words.

In redemptive suffering, we may unite our suffering with that of the Cross of Jesus Christ, as Saint John Paul II explains in his encyclical, *Salvifica Doloris*. We may also offer up our suffering for the redemption of our sins, and the sins of others. Finally, we can offer up our pain, in prayer, for the poor souls in purgatory[85] to be cleansed of their sins.[86]

---

[85] "A state of final purification after death and before entrance into heaven for those who died in God's friendship, but were only imperfectly purified; a final cleansing of human imperfection before one is able to enter the joy of heaven (1031; cf. 1472)." Glossary of the *Catechism of the Catholic Church*, under Purgatory.
[86] CCC 634 and 1032

We also pray especially for those souls in purgatory who have no one to pray for them.

When my ex-husband passed away, I became a widow in the eyes of the Catholic Church because I did not remarry after I was divorced. An annulment was no longer needed. It meant that I would be eligible to make first vows on March 25, 2015. I waited for another nine months. This would be the second year of waiting to make first vows.

The town I lived in after I left Texas was Young Harris, Georgia. From the time I arrived, to the time I made my first vows, I immersed myself in ministries of mercy in the Blairsville, Georgia area. The ministries I worked in were hospital chaplaincy, prison ministry, homebound ministry, and Saint Vincent de Paul Society ministry. I will share in more detail about ministries in the next chapter of this book.

The time finally came to travel to Tijuana, Mexico, to make my first vows.

I arrived at the San Diego airport, which is the airport we fly into every year when we come together for our annual events in Tijuana. Sisters come over the border to pick up sisters who live in the United States, and drive us back over the border to our Tijuana location.

While I was waiting at the baggage claim for my ride, a woman and I began to chat. She was waiting for her daughter. *She told me she was carrying her husband's ashes.* She was responsible for arranging her husband's funeral in San Diego.

She was wrestling with why all this was happening to her. What I found interesting was that I too, before meeting her, was also asking God why he took my ex-husband when he did.

We had a long talk about how it is that God is the only one who knows why and when we wrestle with these things. We are given tests of faith, patience, and perseverance throughout our lives as we deal with difficult challenges.

Do we turn to God when we are going through tough times, to lean on him, and ask for help? Or do we dwell in our sorrow for extended periods of time? She and I were grateful for the conversation. We hugged each other goodbye. I said I would keep her, her daughter, and her husband, in my prayers.

God brought two widows together to console each another. It is amazing how he works.

I arrived in Tijuana several weeks before vows, to work in the Tijuana Federal Penitentiary. Each year I arrived early so that I could work in the prison and help the sisters who live in Tijuana. Working in the prison has always been joyful. Once, there were ten men who remembered me, and I remembered them from previous years of ministry. It brought them joy to see someone they recognized, *who would come back to visit them.*

During this visit to the prison, I talked with an inmate who was arrested the night before. He was in a holding cell with other inmates. He showed me his broken leg, especially to see that it was only bandaged. There was no cast.

The sister I worked with that day informed the infirmary staff of this man's medical issue, so his leg would be adequately cared for. Many of the inmates in this area of the prison, brought in the night before, have not yet received medical attention. It is difficult to see them bruised and bloodied, some with swollen eyes and dried blood coming from their ears, along with cuts and swollen areas.

I am surprised I did not faint at the sight of some of these things, because I have a history of fainting! God's grace got me through it. There is no logical reason for me to have been able to see these atrocities without fainting, if it weren't for God's grace being present. It was the same when I worked in hospital ministry, going into one room after another for almost five years, and not fainting at the sight of blood, and other unpleasant-looking medical conditions.

God, through the graces he gives us to fulfill his will for us, frees us from what would have otherwise held us back from serving those who suffer – our fears, the stench, and the physical and mental suffering that is found in some prisons and hospitals. When we minister, it is as though these things are a lesser concern, because again, our lives are not about us, they are about those we visit, to minister and listen to. *This is only one way God gives us freedom. We learn to humble ourselves to serve those who suffer.*

Time was drawing near to make my first vows.

While I was washing my clothes two nights before vows, and everyone had gone to bed, something unusual happened. I was standing in front of the washing machine waiting for the water to fill up, to add the detergent. *I felt something slowly brush across the whole area of my back.* I was not afraid at first. I turned around and saw that no one was there. Then I became fearful and hurried up the stairs to my room. In retrospect, I believe this was Mother Antonia letting me know she was with me. I realized there was no reason to be afraid.

Then something else happened unexpectedly.

Early in the morning of our first vows, the other candidate, Sister Elaine, and I, were talking in the kitchen. Several large vases of flowers in water were sitting on the kitchen table all night, that would be taken to the reception on this day of our vows.

During our conversation, *one of the vases suddenly fell to the floor*, and water went everywhere with flowers strewn about the floor! We were stunned since the vases had been there all night, and there was no one near the vases to accidently nudge them to fall. No one had walked by either, to cause the vase to suddenly fall to the floor. We cleaned up the water and flowers.

Finally, later in the morning, Sister Elaine and I were walking to the church to make our first vows. A stray dog we had never seen before, walked with us. There are a lot of stray cats and dogs in Tijuana. The dog was skin-and-bones and dirty. We were also concerned he might be rabid. We kept walking and praying along the way, hoping we would arrive safely at the church. We were fine. Nothing happened.

There is quite a lot of planning and effort involved in the annual vows and reception that follows. Usually, the Archbishop of Tijuana celebrates the Mass along with at least three priests. A Mariachi band provides the beautiful church music. It is a bilingual service with some readings in English, and the rest of the Mass in Spanish. Sometimes the homily is bilingual as well, if the person giving the homily is bilingual.

Aside from a few strange things happening—which I understand is normal, because the evil one does not want us to be successful—my day of first vows was glorious. I was a little nervous. I waited longer than anyone else, due to the lack of annulment, so I was ready to make my vows.

At the proper time, Sister Elaine and I proceeded to the front of the church to make our vows for the first time. This is a huge church with open doors to the public, continual street noise, and people streaming in and out of the church.

We recited our vows, received the *Divine Office*[87] prayer book, the cross, cap, and veil. Our vows were received by the General Leader at that time, Sister Judith.

---

[87] *Christian Prayer: The Liturgy of the Hours*, English Translation Prepared by the International Commission on English in the Liturgy, Catholic Book Publishing Co. New York, 1976.

We make the vows of poverty, chastity, obedience, and divine love.

The vow of poverty in our association does not require us to live necessarily in an austere way; however, we may, if we wish. We live more simply, though. We are allowed to own a house with a mortgage, or pay rent. We are financially and individually responsible for our lodging, including if we need a retirement home later. One is not provided for us.

The vow of chastity means we remain chaste, having no intimate or sexual relations with anyone. Jesus is my best friend. He is all I need.

This is a good place to address sexual preference for a moment. There is a common myth in our society that nuns are lesbians. This may be true for some nuns within orders and congregations, as it is likely true for some women throughout the rest of our society. For the record, I have never been a lesbian.

Regarding the vow of obedience, we obey God first, and the General Leader of our association as well. We must also obey the bishop of the diocese in which we reside.

Finally, we make the vow of divine love, as we promise to love others as God loves us.

Reading the vows we make, I especially love these particular words, "I put my talents, my will, my life, to the service of others to manifest to them the charity, and the mercy of God. Jesus Christ, my Savior, teach me your way. Holy Spirit accompany me, enlighten me, and complete in me what I have promised, for the glory of God the Father."

Sister Elaine and I returned to our pew. Afterwards, we were advised to walk up the stairs, to the altar area, to thank the archbishop. Like little school girls, we dutifully left the pew and walked up to thank him, kissed his ring, and returned to our pew!

After this, I remember beaming with joy, looking up at the suspended Crucifix of Jesus Christ over the altar, and whispering to him quietly, "Jesus, we finally did it! I finally made my vows, and I am a Catholic sister! We finally did it!" I was so filled with joy at that moment that my eyes began to fill with tears.

Eudist Servants of the Eleventh Hour group picture with the Archbishop of Tijuana, Archbishop Rafael Romo Muñoz. Vows Day – 2015 – Tijuana, Mexico.
Front row L-R: Sisters Marie Thérèse, Lillian, Nelida, Janice, Mary, Carmen, San Juanita, Anne Marie, Rita
Back row L-R: Sisters Mary Lawrence, Clare, John Mary, Judith, Elaine, Mary Francis, Mariangeles, Viola, Juanita
Knights: Left – John O'Connor; Right – Michael O'Hara
Priests: Left – Father John Boettcher; Right – Father Ricardo Juarez Frausto
(Photo by Francisco Gracia)

After vows were made and Mass was over, everyone walked to the reception location, which was held down the street at a local public facility that was rented for the occasion.

The food was delicious, including a cake that Sister Elaine and I cut together. Young girls wearing beautiful costumes danced the traditional local dances of their culture.

It was a glorious day, one that I waited for a long time. By the grace of God, I finally fulfilled the calling of Jesus to become a Catholic sister, five years after the calling.

The annual assembly meeting was held the next day. All sisters were required to attend.

During the assembly meeting, a sister shared about an unexplained event that happened to her. She said she was praying outside of Mother Antonia's bedroom, which now has a locked glass door, to protect her relics. She said that mother (then deceased) told her to find the white book (a Lenten booklet), and to turn to the page of May 10th. She found the white book in the kitchen and went to this page. May 10th was Mother's Day.[88]

The summary for that day was of Mother Antonia Brenner, our foundress. We were all so pleasantly surprised to learn of this!

After the annual events with my sisters were over, I traveled back to Georgia. A man insisted on helping me get my luggage off the baggage carousel. He was accommodating.

Another man saw me walking to find where my shuttle van was parked. He came up to me to ask if he could help me get to my destination. I said what I was looking for, and he directed me to the right place. He was accommodating.

Another man sat next to me on the shuttle bus. We talked about the Middle East, the evil in the world, the Bible, and many other subjects. He thanked me for all that I do. He

---

[88] "The White Book" refers to a small Lenten booklet published each year by the Diocese of Saginaw. The entry for May 10, 2015 was titled "Mother Superior was a Nun." To learn more about these booklets visit *www.littlebooks.org*.

attended a Catholic school and remembered how the nuns instilled discipline in him, including the use of a ruler on his knuckles. I said I was sorry that this happened to him, even though I was *not* the person who harmed him. Then he laughed, insisting this was good for him!

When we become sisters with the Eudist Servants of the Eleventh Hour, we are required to wear the cap and veil at all times in public. Our hair cannot show. Because of this, I made the drastic change of cutting off my hair, because I realized there was no reason to keep it any longer.

My granddaughter, Olivia, and my son, Joey, buzzed off my hair the first time. They used barber clippers I purchased several years before, in anticipation of when I would become a sister.

At first, it was strange not having hair, but I have gotten used to it, and honestly do not miss it! I loved how liberating it was to get rid of it - no hair gel, no hair spray, no hairdryer, and no haircuts.

I save a lot of money as I simplify my life.

Not having much hair on my head, I went through an adjustment of getting used to the cold in winter. I wear soft cotton head covers when I am at home—the same that are worn by those who have had chemotherapy and lost their hair—to keep my head warm. My sister, Jackie, gave me one, then I ordered two more. One of the Blairsville prison ministry team members, Linda, knitted a warm cap for the colder temperatures of winter and gave it to me. I appreciated these caps very much!

Once I returned home, the Knights of Columbus and Saint Vincent de Paul Society volunteers of the church I belonged to at the time, gave me a lovely reception in the parish hall. This was to celebrate becoming a Catholic sister. My son, granddaughter, brother, sister and her family, were able to attend. Their presence was especially thoughtful that day. The reception was very considerate of my church and unexpected.

The parishioners were genuinely happy for me, that I finally made my vows. They knew how long I waited to do this. It seemed as though they were agonizing right along with me at times. I notice it is the same when a man is on a journey to become a deacon or priest. The whole congregation walks with him. There have been many seminarians we walked with along the way, who received our heart-felt prayers. *These men need our daily prayers.* It was the same with me. They offered their daily prayers for a woman called late-in-life to become a consecrated sister. *I needed their prayers!*

Each Catholic parish is a family.

Picture taken a month after first vows – 2015
(Picture taken at the reception by my granddaughter, Olivia Power)

My pastor at the time allowed me to give a fifteen-minute talk about the journey, during the reception. Now he and I have a running joke about how I did not limit my speech as we had discussed, because the speech I gave was forty-five minutes! I just *could not* stop talking about the journey, because there were so many details to share.

During Eucharistic Adoration one day, soon after I made my vows, I heard Jesus tell me, "How could you have ever doubted me?" This statement is a humbling one for anyone who has ever heard his voice.

Shortly after I returned to Georgia, I met with the Vicar of Women Religious at the Atlanta Archdiocese and my priest, to introduce myself in-person as a new sister in the diocese. A letter had been previously mailed from my General Leader to the Archbishop, introducing me to the diocese. Any time a sister relocates from one diocese to another, a letter from our General Leader must be forwarded to the bishop of the gaining diocese to introduce her.

Here are a couple more pictures that were taken after first vows.

Visiting my mother, a month after first vows – 2015. Mom was the most selfless person I ever knew. May she rest in peace.
(Picture taken by my sister-in-law, Julie McDonald)

Enjoying the park with my granddaughter,
Olivia Power, and my son – 2015
(Picture taken by my son, Joey Power)

Walking with one of my sons, Christopher Power – 2015
(Photo taken by Steve Hellwich)

Traveling in the North Carolina mountains, in 2015, capturing the glory of God, knowing he will always be my focus and strength, and that he's got my back. This was the first selfie I had ever taken. As you can see, I did not do it right! *This picture though, says so much about him, not me, which is the way it should be. The picture turned out exactly the way he wanted it to. Glorious.*

Cleaning windows of the church – 2016
(Picture taken by Annette Dinelli)

Picture taken with Mother Antonia Brenner's picture - 2018

As a final statement on making first vows, it was a glorious day!

> *Question for the reader to contemplate: Can I see myself on a journey like this?*

CHAPTER 11

PRISON MINISTRY AND OTHER MINISTRIES OF MERCY

―⁄⁄⧫⧫―

Our foundress, Mother Antonia Brenner, gave us the best example of prison ministry and service to the poor in Tijuana, Mexico. We follow her spirituality as well as that of our patron saint, Saint John Eudes, as we minister to the least of our brothers and sisters.

Mother performed spiritual and corporal works of mercy, just as the sisters in Tijuana still do today. Although the sisters do spiritual works too, much of the work is corporal works of mercy, giving inmates and the poor much-needed items, the necessities.

The corporal works of mercy are feeding the hungry, sheltering the homeless, clothing the naked, visiting the sick and imprisoned, and burying the dead. The spiritual works of mercy are instructing, advising, consoling, and comforting.[89]

Most of the work performed by the majority of our sisters in the United States are spiritual works of mercy, although some corporal works take place as well. It is different for

---

[89] CCC 2447

every sister, depending upon where she is, and the ministries she works in.

In both countries, sisters serve those God brings to them, listening, praying, and being still for a moment to listen to their dilemmas.

One of my favorite quotes from Mother Antonia is, "There are three ways to get into heaven. Be kind, be kind, and be kind." We use this simple wisdom in our ministries. Although it is sometimes challenging to be kind to those who mock and persecute us because of our faith, we strive to become kinder each day.

The sisters and I are mindful that our ministries are never about us. Our focus is on the people standing in front of us, focusing on their needs, not ours. We strive to be patient and compassionate when listening to someone's troubles—to just be there for them.

While I listen to the suffering Christ (the imprisoned or poor) standing in front of me, I am, at the same time, listening to the Holy Spirit, asking for guidance and wisdom on how to help them. They need help with many things, depending upon their situations. I share with them what I hear from the Holy Spirit. Sometimes he simply has me share my own experiences with them, and other times, he gives me *good words* I cannot believe came out of my own mouth. This is evangelizing at its best. This tells me I am digesting the Word of God, the gospels of God, through his beloved son, Jesus Christ, and given to me.

Doing ministry with someone does not always involve talking. Ministry can merely be a silent presence.

"Sitting *Shiva*," an old Jewish custom during the mourning of a loved one, is an excellent example of how we can simply be present for someone. There is no need to speak, to inquire, or do anything at all. Just be. Be there for them, nothing else.[90]

Similarly, as Christians, we go into the silence with someone during a time of loss, just as Psalm 46:10 reminds us to be still and know God. It is in the silence we find him and come to know and understand him.

Using the virtues we learn in formation—humility, patience, and perseverance—we minister in hospital chaplaincy, pray with the poor, do hospice work, immigration work, and assist with pastoral duties, as we can. We listen to strangers we meet in public, and we pray with them.

God either brings them to us, or he brings us to them.

Prison ministry is the primary ministry of the Eudist Servants of the Eleventh Hour. *After we become sisters, we are expected to work in prison ministry, in-person.* This is the expectation, whether we work in Tijuana or the United States.

We believe God protects us when we do ministry. The only time I am a little anxious is when I am starting at a facility for the first time. This is because I do not yet know the layout of the place, the guards, and the inmates. Once I start doing prison ministry in a facility, I am just fine.

One of the most anxious times I had was starting at the Tijuana Federal Penitentiary in Mexico. There were so many gated entry areas, corridors, and cells. I knew there were dangerous cartel members housed there; however, the prison is very well managed, with many alert guards, and strict rules.

The most fearful time I had when starting prison ministry at a location, was when I met with a death row inmate for the first time at the Georgia Classification and Diagnostic Prison in Jackson, Georgia, in 2019. The fear I experienced

---

[90] To learn more about this custom, visit www.shiva.com/learning-center/understanding/.

was from Satan, as usual. *I prayed my way through it like I usually do.* Once I saw the smile on the inmate's face when I first met him, the fear disappeared immediately. I knew I was there to fulfill God's calling for me, to serve those who suffer. God was in charge once again!

Now I visit the Catholics on death row, as well as the incarcerated law enforcement officers. It is always a joy to spend time with them as I know I am with the least of our brothers. These visits bring joy to God. Through his son, Jesus, he tells us to visit those in prison (Mt. 25:35-45). It's not a suggestion. *To be there for someone in their darkest time is a joy for those of us who are prison chaplains.* And prisoners genuinely appreciate our time with them.

After doing prison ministry in Texas, Mexico, and Georgia, I have to say that the most joyful prison ministry I have experienced was at the Colwell Probation Detention Center of the Georgia Department of Corrections, Blairsville, Georgia. After I moved to north Georgia, I inquired about becoming a volunteer at their facility. Diane Hassett, the superintendent at the time, approved me to begin a prison ministry program at her facility. I also received approval from the pastor of my church and the archdiocese.

Former Superintendent Hassett, Officer Philip Carter, and Secretary Leonda Prentice of the detention center have been the backbone of this successful Rescued Program[91] from its inception, along with other officers, working tirelessly to help men change their lives for the better, while giving rescued dogs a better life too.

Although Ms. Hassett is retired now, she continues her divine calling to lead the Rescued Program volunteers, giving glory to

---

[91] The Facebook page for the Rescued Program can be found at *www.facebook. com/RescuedProgram.*

God through her work for him. God uses her and all the other team members for the sacred work of saving dogs and men.

First and foremost, the men are taught that the meaning of integrity, simply defined, is doing the right thing when no one is watching.

The superintendent determined the type of spirituality program she wanted me to do. She could have decided it would be a Bible study, prayer group, or something else. She thought about it, then gave me the title of the program she had in mind: *Problem Solving with Spirituality.*[92]

There was no existing structure we knew of at the time that I could use as an example of this to follow. She explained that the spirituality program would supplement the Rescued Program of the detention center. Rescued dogs were donated to the center. Inmates were trained on how to train the dogs. The components of the Rescued Program include (at the time of this writing):

- Positive Reinforcement Dog Training Techniques
- On the Job Training (OJT) Certificate in Grooming Central Georgia Technical College
- Problem Solving with Spirituality – Catholic Church
- Georgia Best – Department of Labor – Soft Work Skills – Resume and Portfolios/Interviewing Techniques
- Basic Animal Health Class and Pet First Aid and CPR

---

[92] Three programs were developed for *Problem Solving with Spirituality.* The first two programs were developed and copyrighted by me. Our team and I then developed handouts for the third program and included the use of Rob Bell's NOOMA collection of DVDs. The DVDs may be purchased at *www.faithgateway.com/products/nooma-complete-collection.* These are not Catholic-produced DVDs; however, the messages of the pastor are Bible-based and consistent with the teachings of Jesus. Not all facilities have DVD players available for the prison minister's use, and in that case, the first or second program, which still involves small group discussions on similar topics, may be used.

- Worksource Development Career Coach – Resume and Job Searching
- Let Go and Let God – Addiction Advisers Class
- Money Management
- Anger Management
- Integrity
- Probation Expectations
- GED Classes

The *Problem Solving with Spirituality* program she asked me for would have to be created from scratch. To do this, time would need to be spent in Eucharistic Adoration, in prayer. I needed help. The Holy Spirit guided me through the creation of the first program. Before I began work on the program, I prayed. I simply talked with Jesus, asking him to help me develop this program. I gave thanks afterwards, as well. This is the way I approach any project, including writing this book. Pray before, during, and after an effort. The best outcomes happen that way!

To incorporate sustainability of the prison ministry, ensuring we would be present *every* Monday afternoon at the facility, I was permitted by the pastor to establish a prison ministry team. And I was responsible for other demanding ministries in the Blairsville area, so to ensure weekly coverage, establishing a team was important to do.

The team is currently led by a very devoted and compassionate team leader, Anne Parks, who graciously assumed my responsibilities when I relocated to Canton, Georgia. The team continues to do a great job of serving "the imprisoned Christ" and supporting the Rescued Program.

The intent of these specific prison ministry programs is to stimulate thinking in a positive way, to encourage discussion, and to help inmates do the work involved to develop an improved version of themselves, using the values and virtues of Jesus Christ, as applied to their daily challenges.

During a ministry visit, we focus on one topic, such as forgiveness or prayer, for example. A one-page handout of five or six questions on the subject is given to the inmates. Each handout contains related Bible scripture references the inmates may research once they have free personal time.

The programs have been used in six prison and detention center facilities, including Georgia's death row and also with the incarcerated law enforcement officers. *Every place they have been used, they appear to be effective in causing inmates to think differently than they have before, and to contemplate things they may have never considered.*

The Catholic Church in Gilmore County, Ellijay, Georgia, has a team that was led by Greg Altman—another compassionate and devoted team leader—when I worked with his church to start a new prison ministry program, again with the approval of the pastor. At the beginning of the ministry at their local detention center, the first program was used.

The prison ministry team of the Catholic Church in Lilburn, Georgia, that I was a part of, was led by Ann Basile, then by Lisa Olwine, both also compassionate, devoted ministry leaders, who used all three programs at the Gwinnett County Detention Center. These two leaders and the team members facilitated other prison ministry programs through the church as well.

I used the second program in Phillips Prison, Buford, Georgia, a medium-security prison for men, and used all three programs at the Metro Transition Center, Atlanta, Georgia, a facility for women with good behavior, who are on work release programs, and transitioning out of incarcerated life, back to their hometowns.

The programs can be used at other incarcerated facilities as well. There are many other prison ministry programs that have been posted to the internet during recent years. The local Catholic pastor's support is important to have prior to starting a prison ministry, to establish the connection with his local incarcerated flock of the church.

If a pastor can include the local incarcerated facilities in their flock, Catholics can receive their sacraments, just as Catholics in nursing homes and hospitals do. And those who are not Catholic, who might be visited by a priest, would greatly benefit from the invaluable wisdom and spiritual support that a priest could give them.

The pastor does not need to accompany team members every week. Although, it is always a gift from God when a pastor's heart yearns to do prison ministry on a regular basis. When this happens, he will likely accompany the team on a regular basis, and with joy, because he recognizes the gift he is being given to him by God, to serve "the imprisoned Christ."

The team members *must have* a heart for prison ministry and be spiritually grounded in their Christian faith.

The teams decide, with the help of the Holy Spirit, what format and material they will use when ministering to inmates. This can change depending on what the team decides to do, and can also be based on feedback from the inmates themselves. Chaplains of facilities can also be helpful in identifying what type of program may work best.

Ideally, priests and deacons from the local Catholic churches are available to say Mass or provide a Communion Service at incarceration facilities, and administer the Sacraments, if possible. *Priests can hear inmate confessions of Catholics, a very important part of prison ministry, as this helps the inmate reconcile his sins with God.*

I have great admiration for priests who will honor what Jesus tells us in Matthew 25:35-45, which includes visiting those in prison. I personally know priests who will meet with inmates who are not even Catholic, to provide them with spiritual counseling. I have a sincere appreciation for these priests who give of themselves in this way.

Although I cannot say Mass or administer the Sacraments, I have conducted a "Communion Service" for inmates I visit, since I am an Extraordinary Minister of the Eucharist. *It is similar to visiting someone who is homebound, in a nursing home, or hospital.* We reflect on the readings of the day, pray, and offer individual prayers. I deliver Communion to those who are Catholic, and a blessing to those who are not. Of course, I cannot give a final blessing as a priest does at Mass, but I can give them a motherly blessing with holy water as a mother would to a child. The inmates are truly humbled, and appreciate these blessings very much.

We provide Bibles to inmates if we see they are genuinely interested in Bible study. We do not merely hand them out to everyone, because we have learned that sometimes they use them for the wrong reasons. One example of this is that I was told they were only using them as weights in a detention center. They were not reading them. For that reason, I only give a Bible to an inmate if I feel confident that they genuinely want to learn more.

Teaching inmates how to pray, meditate, and reflect on the rosary, is welcomed by some inmates, others not so much. If a group of inmates wishes to learn, it does not matter to me what faith they are. That does not matter. What matters is teaching them yet another way to pray. I give them a rosary made by our church rosary group, as well as a pamphlet on how to pray the rosary. I lead them through the steps, teaching them how to pray it. I also have asked the inmates to pray for the women who have made the rosaries for them.

I have given away many rosaries, in various ministries, not just prison ministry. When I see it most needed is when I meet someone who is in what I call, "the pit of despair." *In our Catholic faith, when we work with desperate people, we know that prayer is an important first step to wellness.* We also refer them to Christian counselors if they have not already met with one.

We teach inmates about prayer. We talk about what prayer is, how to pray, and when to pray. They are usually interested in talking about this subject, as they know this is where the relationship with God begins.

The rosary is made up of prayer beads to help a person pray, meditate, and reflect, regardless of their faith. I have also seen women and men cry when they received a rosary from me, because it reminded them of a grandmother who used to pray for them, using the rosary, and has since passed away. *The rosary can provide consolation and calm to someone who is greatly unsettled about something.*

A few more words about the physical item of the rosary, is that once it is blessed by a priest, deacon, or blessed with holy water by me, for example, it is a blessed item, and should not be sold. It is sacred and is not worn as a piece of jewelry; however, in the Tijuana Federal Penitentiary, and other incarcerated facilities, the men and women wear the rosaries, for fear of them being stolen.

The purpose of Christian prison ministry is to help people come to know Jesus Christ, then help them to apply his values and virtues to their lives. This process can take longer for some people, depending upon where they are in their faith journey. For others, once they are open to learning more about Christianity, their faith grows much more quickly, because they yearn to know more about the way, the truth, and the life of Jesus Christ.

We pray for the creation and implementation of innovative programs in our nation that will give inmates the opportunity to reform themselves, for those who truly want to be reformed. Prisoners are not much different than we are. We are all sinners. There is only one judge. He doesn't measure sin. He is a merciful God for all.

Programs based upon restorative justice show great promise. For willing participants of restorative justice programs, it can be *an opportunity for everyone to heal* from the harm caused by the crime.

Super Soul Sunday is a television series hosted by Oprah Winfrey. On February 18, 2018, she interviewed Shaka Senghor about his book, *Writing My Wrongs: Life, Death and Redemption in an American Prison,* a New York Times bestseller.[93] He shared his spiritual journey, and conversion of heart, mind, and soul. He is a former drug addict and dealer. It was a powerful testimony.

What impressed me the most of his interview, was his discussion of a letter he received from the mother of the man he murdered. *In the letter to Shaka, the mother told him she loved him and forgave him for killing her son. She believed people deserve a second chance at life, and that we need to help inmates reconstruct their lives, not just lock them up.*

The mother of this murdered man provides us with the best example of a practicing Christian who, like Jesus Christ, forgave those who sinned. *This is what we strive to become, a forgiving people.*

The most challenging spiritual work of mercy is working with those who are intellectually challenged in prisons. Many do not receive the medication and treatment they need. We

---

[93] Shaka Senghor, *Writing My Wrongs: Life, Death and Redemption in an American Prison* (New York: Convergent Books, 2016).

need to pray unceasingly for them. We can at least pray that they receive the care they need.

The sad truth about the unique society of prison is that everyone is potentially a victim, especially if they have a drug addiction and are compelled to bargain with their bodies, sexually, in return for illicit drugs to feed their habits. I visited young men with strong addictions in a medium-level security prison who were victims of predators. *I saw a glimpse of hell through these boys' eyes when I met with them.* When a person studies the history of these young men, they may very well find that they came from dysfunctional families which abused drugs, alcohol, and sex.

Maybe they never had a chance growing up, but with God all things are possible, and this is our hope for them.

As a mother, this breaks my heart to see. Women are included in this category too, of course. All of these men and women are someone else's sons and daughters, and many of them are abandoned by their families. Occasionally, we come across a bright light of Christ in someone who is in prison. There is hope for everyone. There is always hope for change, and this is what gives me strength and determination to return to incarcerated facilities. To say it is a challenge to work with these particular inmates is an understatement.

One of the spiritual works of mercy I enjoyed very much was working as a chaplain at the local hospital. The chaplains committed to one seven-day week of duty at a time, visiting sick patients, and mothers of newborn babies. It was a small hospital, well-run, and staffed with caring medical folks.

Another spiritual work God has given me is speaking engagements. I was not prepared for this, as this was not part of my formation. This was another idea of God's I was not too excited about, but I accepted it, because it is a *good fruit of the Holy Spirit.* Following prayer, meditation, and discernment, I have accepted invitations to serve as a speaker.

The first speaking invitation was for the Atlanta Archdiocese Catholic Council of Women, to speak on the subject of spirituality. I agreed to do this, not knowing how many women would be present. I knew nothing about this group of women, or how large their group was, and learned later what a wonderful group of women they were.

About halfway through developing my PowerPoint presentation, I asked how many women would attend. I was informed the answer was 113 women! I had never given a presentation to that many people. Little did I know that this would prepare me for giving talks to larger groups later.

As a member of the Georgia Catholics Against the Death Penalty,[94] I gave a five-minute talk after all the weekend Masses at my church, about ending the Death Penalty in Georgia. If you live in Georgia or any other state that still has the death penalty, please contact your legislators to ask them to end this unjust, immoral, archaic practice, which when carried out, interferes with the ongoing redemptive work God is trying to do with death row inmates.

If your legislators say they are pro-life, ask them to define that for you.

I would be terribly remiss if I did not ask everyone to please always pray for victims of crime (especially heinous crime), and their families. Unless we have been in the shoes of a family member of a victim, who has lost them to a heinous crime, we will never comprehend the depth of their loss. But one thing we can do for the families is to pray for them. Pray that they will be consoled in the loss of their loved ones, taken much too soon from this life. *It is difficult*

---

[94] For more information, go to www.gacadp.org.

to understand why God would allow heinous crimes to happen to his own divine creations. I believe he will tell us this answer when we get to heaven. In the meantime, please pray for the victims and their families, prisoners and their families, for forgiveness of those who committed heinous crimes, and peace for everyone involved.

God has a way of preparing us for whatever he wants us to do next. He builds on our experience to use for the next endeavor he asks us to do. That is just the way he works, from what I have witnessed.

There were other groups of women, mostly Women's Guilds of Catholic churches in the Atlanta Archdiocese, who invited me to speak. At one church in particular in Newnan, Georgia, I conducted a Day of Reflection for eighty women that was composed of four, 15-minute talks. It was a glorious day with wonderful spiritually-grounded women.

It was a workshop that gave women the opportunity to work on their conversions of heart, mind, and soul. The women of this church were very welcoming and kind. They even celebrated an accompanying sister's (Sister Eileen) birthday with a surprise birthday cake! It was a beautiful day, full of Christian fellowship.

And I have led St. Vincent de Paul Society council-led day retreats for Vincentian members with a focus on topics of spirituality. These are beautiful opportunities to enjoy the camaraderie of fellow Vincentians as well, with a focus on spiritual growth.

Whether we are doing corporal or spiritual works of mercy, we are often with one person at a time. Each interaction is unique and orchestrated by God himself.

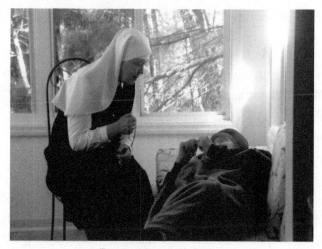

Praying the rosary with a
St. Vincent de Paul Society client/neighbor – 2017
(Picture taken by Vincentian Nami Byers)

In Matthew 18:12-14, we are reminded of how the shepherd leaves his flock to go after one who has gone astray. *He leaves the rest of the flock alone and unattended to do this.* This is pretty unbelievable, isn't it? That is how much God truly loves each and every divine creation.

Let me give you a good example of this scripture reflection. Prison ministers in the Atlanta area, including myself, have driven almost two hours, one way, to visit sometimes only one inmate at a facility. At some facilities, we never know how many inmates will attend our service because it is voluntary attendance.

For us, the drive, rush hour traffic, pouring rain, dangerous locations, and putting our lives at risk is worth that one person we see. *Faith is not always logical or reasonable. Until a person develops strong faith through serving the marginalized, one cannot know or understand the joy that comes with the ministry that drives us.*

The ministries I have done since I joined the Eudist Servants have been joyful and fulfilling. In my former life, I never planned to work in these ministries. *These ministries were God's ideas, not mine.* Now that I have been introduced to the ministries by him, I am so grateful to God for showing me.

God could be using this book to communicate with you. Is he?

One final type of ministry we might do after we are vowed sisters is working in leadership and administrative roles for our association. When a sister works in one of these roles, it is her primary ministry, as she is committed to helping our association of sisters and new candidates. She may also be involved in prison ministry and other ministries of mercy, as was our foundress, Mother Antonia Brenner.

After I made my first vows, I returned home. Shortly afterward, I began to receive the calling to start a discernment house, to help women to (1) discern their callings, (2) prepare for formation in Tijuana, Mexico, and (3) help them with their transformation into the consecrated life as a Catholic sister. My General Leader, Vicar, and Archbishop, approved of this endeavor. I developed a structured curriculum to keep me and the potential candidates focused.

Facilitating a discernment house, which normally had only one woman present, sometimes two, and occasionally a woman who was visiting, was added to my existing duties of (1) pre-screening women by email and phone calls for consideration to join our association, (2) secretary for the association for three years, (3) prison ministry team leader, (4) Saint Vincent de Paul Society conference spiritual advisor, and (5) hospital chaplain duty.

This was too much for me, but I did not know it until I experienced a major warning sign. One night I had atrial fibrillation of the heart, more commonly known as AFIB.

My heart was doing aerobics. My breathing was adversely affected, and I was light-headed and weak. I went to the emergency room. They fixed me up. I am on medicine to control this now, and I just keep going, keeping in mind that at times, I need to rest.

What is interesting about this is that I believed I was supposed to start a discernment house to help other middle-aged women, I went about the work to do this, and God opened the doors. *Then change happened. I am no longer running a discernment house because I realized through prayer that I could not abandon the people I was serving in prison ministry, at the hospital, and the poor in the area. Something had to go.*

What I have discerned, through prayer, is that God showed me my limitations, that I cannot do everything. I am only one person. I felt as though I failed in that area of responsibility.

It is the same feeling of failure when we work with a client/neighbor, a stranger, or a patient, and they are not open to the word of God, or the promise of eternal life in heaven. We realize then, that we are not meant to bring every person we meet to the cross of Jesus Christ. For those who are not open, we surrender them to God, and let go of them. We pray for them, that they will find their way, and that God will surround them with spiritually grounded people to help them.

Everyone has their own journey with God.

Questions for the reader to contemplate: Do I wonder what God might have in store for me? What is he waiting for me to do? Am I placing obstacles in front of myself, that are keeping me from moving forward? Have I turned away from God's plan for me, doing instead what I want to do?

CHAPTER 12
COLLECTION OF PERSONAL STORIES

꼭

Many unexplained and sometimes mystical events have happened along the way of my journey. This chapter is a collection of some of those stories. Some are happy and joyful, while others are sad. Some of these stories happened with witnesses, some without. All are true.

Are You a Jewish Nun?

Checking out at the register, a man asked me, "Are you a Jewish nun?" My response was, "No, I am a Catholic sister." I am sure he asked me that because there is a Star of David affixed to the cross I wear. I love to share the history of the cross we wear. Initially, a Tijuana Federal Penitentiary inmate made the cross for Mother Antonia Brenner, our foundress. She added the Star of David pendant to the cross of nails to remind people that Jesus was Jewish and also to never forget the Holocaust. Strangers are interested in the cross and they typically say, "That's a beautiful cross you are wearing." I also like to say that it is a good symbol of the relationship between the Old Testament and the New Testament.

Are You a Nun?

A stranger called out to me in a store parking lot, "Excuse me, ma'am, are you a nun?" We spent a few minutes chatting. My granddaughter, Olivia, was with me. She waited patiently while I spoke with him. He thought I was her aunt, but I corrected him to say I am her grandmother. He said how much the nuns meant to him when he was younger and going to Catholic school. I asked if there was something I could pray for, for him. He said he is selfish, always thinking of himself, and wants to get better about praying - he already knew what areas he needed to work on. Then I told him that the best thing we older people can do is to stand up for Jesus, to go out and invest our time and energy in the younger generations because they are the future of this country. Many are lost, and do not have a foundation of faith or of the higher power, God.

Army of Angels

One of our parishioners was residing at a seniors' facility for temporary care. I was asked to take the Eucharist to her. As I approached the front desk, the woman who was sitting there jumped back in her chair when she saw me walk into the lobby of the facility. I was not sure why she reacted that way until later in our conversation. After I told her why I was there, she said she needed to share something with me. I wondered what this would be about.

She began by saying that she felt a good presence from me when I walked into the facility. Well, I had heard that before, but what she told me next was something I was never told. She said that when I walked in, there was an army of angels around me!

God sends his angels to help us through difficult and challenging times, and some people have a special gift to actually see them with their eyes. This woman was a genuine, sincere, good, Christian woman, who wanted to share with me what she experienced when I arrived at her facility. I had no reason to doubt what she told me.

It is comforting to know I am accompanied by God's angels to do his work.

Atrial Fibrillation – AFIB

I was hospitalized with AFIB when my heart started doing aerobics. My breathing was irregular, and I was weak. My heart corrected itself naturally by the end of the day, going back into a regular rhythm on its own without taking medicine to correct it.

Throughout the day, the medical staff entered my room to check on me. If I was awake, they would look at the medical monitor and say, "You have not 'converted' yet." I was so curious about this statement and thought about it all day.

That evening, a nurse looked at the medical monitor while she and I were talking, and she said, "You converted!" With great emphasis, I replied, "Well, yes I have!"

The next day I told all the medical staff who visited me, the story of how I *thought* they were talking about my *spiritual conversion*. They laughed when they learned my reaction to them using the word, "conversion," when they referred to how I was doing.

I was thinking to myself, that, well, yes, I had a spiritual conversion, so what were they talking about? Of course, they were referring to my heart converting back to the normal rhythm, whereas, I was talking about having a conversion of heart, mind, and soul. Terminology. I still laugh about this.

Boy at the Airport

As I was walking to my gate at the airport, I saw a boy about nine years old out of the corner of my eye. He was running sideways, doing what looked like a football game end-run to meet up with me at an intersecting point in front of me, or so it seemed. He never lost eye contact with me as he was running. I am surprised he and I did not accidently run into someone! As he got close, he lifted his hand. He wanted to high-five me! He looked over at his parents after we high-fived each other, who were standing close by, watching. I glanced over to them and smiled. I said to the boy, "God bless you!" We both then went our separate ways.

Consoling a Grieving Inmate

I received a call from Ms. Diane Hassett, the superintendent of a detention center at the time, asking me to meet with an inmate. His eleven-week-old infant had died of sudden infant death syndrome (SIDS). His wife was alone when she found the dead baby in the crib. He was very distraught. He fought back the tears the entire time we met, and so did I. I let the Holy Spirit guide me in what to say to him and how to console him. Jesus told me to tell this young man to borrow a Bible from someone in the detention center. He said he knew of someone in his cell who could lend him one. At the time, I did not have one with me to give him. I asked him to randomly thumb through the Bible to pick a scripture that speaks to him, write it at the top of a piece of paper, and meditate about it.

Then I asked him to write his thoughts about the scripture and mail these reflections to his wife. I also encouraged him to ask her to do the same thing for him. I explained that since they could not be together, to console one another, that the scriptures might help to form a connection of some sort, writing to one another about what God tells them through scriptures. He and his wife were used to reading the Bible anyway. Also, if they wrote to each other, this would be something special to look forward to each day. Their communication, with Bible scripture as their focus, might help a little bit with the loss of their baby, and their separation as well.

I realized the Holy Spirit was helping me, to help them learn how to lean on their faith during this tragic time in their lives.

Before my meeting was over with him, the Holy Spirit/Jesus also told me to share with him that sometimes God just wants little flowers for his garden, meaning, little children. I also shared that his baby's spirit would always be with him and his wife.

I learned several days later that he was granted permission to go to the funeral with an armed guard.

When I recall this event and write about it, my heart is saddened again, thinking of the pain I saw in his face and thinking of how painful it was for his wife to find the child as it was. I prayed for all of them during their time of loss.

Before I arrived to meet with him, I did not know what I was going to say to him or how to console him. I relied entirely upon the Holy Spirit because I have never personally experienced this type of loss. I was grateful to finally have a strong Christian faith at this point in my life to be able to help him.

Contractor

I was waiting on the front porch one morning for a contractor to arrive. As he was getting out of his truck, a complete stranger, he saw me and said, "Sister, I've been waiting so long to meet you!" I said, "Well, I have been waiting to meet you, too!" I welcomed him into my home to do some repairs, and we had a lively conversation about faith, life, wrong choices, forgiveness, stress, prayer, and many other areas he and I wanted to discuss. He was so excited about our exchange that he forgot a $1,000 (he estimated) piece of equipment when he left for the day, and he came back several weeks later to retrieve it. When he returned to pick up his equipment, I gave him a daily devotional book, *Jesus Calling*,[95] suggesting that he read and reflect on one page a day to help him in his journey of faith. He was seeking answers and he was open and receptive to learning more about the Christian faith.

Courageous Drug Addict

Shortly after I started working in prison ministry at the Metro Atlanta Transition Center for Women in Atlanta,

---

[95] Sarah Young, *Jesus Calling* (Nashville, Tennessee: Thomas Nelson, 2004).

Georgia, a small group of women and I were talking about preparing to transition from incarcerated life to home life. We were doing this to help them prepare mentally, spiritually, and emotionally before returning to their hometowns.

Each woman was asked to share what type of home environment they would return to. Almost all the women spoke of having supportive family members. One woman, however, told us she could not go back to live with her family because, unfortunately, *her family was the problem*. She said that her entire family of drug addicts was a bad influence on her.

That night she told us how she made the courageous and challenging decision to completely cut ties with her family for now, to allow her to have the chance to make a better life for herself. It could become a life that was sober, spiritual, and joyful. She set goals for herself to become a better version of herself.

In prison ministry, we encourage men and women to identify whom they can no longer associate with when they return home, due to the possible influence of the things that feed their addictions. We also discuss the possible return to prison if they do not prepare themselves for resisting these temptations, when returning home.

The person in their hometown who might be a negative influence, could be a family member or a childhood friend of twenty years, for example. If a person is serious about changing their lives for the better, and doing the work that comes with it, they stand a better chance of succeeding, if they avoid these old negative relationships.

I inform inmates not to be too afraid or too proud to ask for help as they try to get on their feet after incarceration. I advise them to go to churches, Saint Vincent de Paul Society, and other charity organizations in their areas, asking for help. So often, many of them have been abandoned entirely by their families. They also have a criminal record which can limit their employment opportunities. Society could—and should—be more helpful in giving someone a second chance. After all, we have made mistakes too. Chances are, someone gave *us* a second chance.

In Appendix C of this book, you will find a helpful, thorough document, created by Charles and Linda Johnston of the *Let Go and Let God Addiction Adviser* program of the Colwell Detention Center Rescued Program in Blairsville, Georgia. The handout is entitled *Problem Solving with Spirituality – Transition from Incarcerated to Home.*[96] It was developed for this program when Charles and Linda were originally part of our team, before they began their own separate and successful ministry. This resource has been given to many inmates who are *preparing* to go home. It has been distributed to inmates in other incarcerated facilities through my prison ministry as well. The discussions that are outlined in this document help an inmate mentally, spiritually, and emotionally to prepare for leaving incarcerated life and return to their hometowns. *Making needed changes is critical to their success. If no changes are made, chances are they will return to incarcerated life.*

Department Store Employee

This department store was always a busy place. Many things happened there that people were not even aware of. On one particular day, I said hello to an employee I met there before. We greeted each other with smiles, asking, "How are you?" This time though, she choked back tears, could barely speak, and said, "*I am hanging from His Heart.*" She was speaking of

---

[96] Charles and Linda Johnston, *Problem Solving with Spirituality Program*, 2014. See Appendix C.

Jesus Christ himself. We both instantly became teary-eyed. We could not talk, so we hugged.

In some inexplicable way, we had an unspoken understanding of one another. I cared very much about whatever it was she was going through. And her expression told me she appreciated that I cared. She had to get back to work and walked away. I went on with my day as well. I still think about her and pray for her. Every once in a while, I ask about her at the store, and usually I am told that they do not know anyone by the description I give them of her. They tell me that she may not work there anymore. *God knows who she is, and how she is doing.*

Detention Center Inmate

When we began working with a new group of inmates at a detention center, an inmate shared with us that he is Buddhist. After a few of our Christian sessions with him, he said, "Well, I'm not so sure that I am Buddhist." He was raised Catholic. He was seeking answers, and was happy to return to his childhood foundation of the Catholic faith.

Dying Friend

A man stopped me as I entered the grocery store. He said he wanted to say hello, then to share the reason he wanted to talk to me. He began to tell me that recently he visited a very good friend of his in the hospital, who was dying. In her last hours, he held her in his arms as she died. He was slightly weeping as he shared this with me. My eyes became weepy as well, as I listened to his experience of losing his dear friend. I reassured him that his friend would always be with him in spirit and that she is resting peacefully now. I hugged him, bade him farewell, and held both of them in prayer.

Dying Man Wanting to Let Go

When I was a hospital chaplain, I had the opportunity to visit an elderly man in the hospital who had cancer and had fallen at home. When he was admitted, he informed the staff that he wanted to refuse food and water—that he wanted to die. According to him, when he asked them how long it would take to die without any nourishment, they told him it would take about five days.

His wife was by his side every day until he died. She was Catholic. He was not. When I met them, I told her I would bring her the Eucharist (Jesus) every day, since I was going to Mass each day. And so, I did. I also prayed with both of them.

What I did not realize at the beginning of these visits was how much he wanted to pass on, but that she did not want him to leave her. He was calm and accepting of his situation. She was very distraught about the situation and was *not* ready for him to pass. When I visited them, most of the time I ministered to her, as he would be sleeping.

What I witnessed, though, was what can happen when a spouse communicates her unwillingness to let go of a dying partner, and because of this, the dying spouse suffers even more. He held on as long as he could to satisfy his wife. She was physically in pain from her own afflictions as well. I encouraged her to be seen by her doctor.

It was thirty days before he died.

Dying Patient

The Chief of Chaplains asked me to visit a man in the hospital. When we visit someone in the hospital, we usually do not know their medical history or even the reason for hospitalization. I opened the door to his room to find that this man was missing limbs. He had been in an unfortunate motorcycle accident over thirty years ago and spent the last thirty years in a nursing home. I was unaware of his medical condition before I visited him. He shared with me that he had diabetes and cancer, and that *he was dying*.

I asked him, "What can I pray for, for you?" He told me he believed Jesus would not take him to heaven until he asked for forgiveness for *all of his sins*. He was afraid he could not remember all of his sins, and that because of this, Jesus would not take him to heaven. He asked me if I could help him with that. He had tears in his eyes and had a look of total anguish on his face. While he was speaking to me, I was, of course, also listening to the Holy Spirit of God, listening for direction and guidance on what to tell this man.

What I heard from the Holy Spirit was this: I was to tell him that God is a merciful God and forgives all sins. I said that he should ask God to forgive him for *all* of his sins, even the ones he cannot remember, and that if he is genuinely sorry, God will forgive him.

He told me that after the motorcycle accident, he was lying on the ground. The driver of the other car, a young woman, came over and said to him, "Look what you have done to my car!" He said he looked up and saw his limbs lying around him when she came up and said this to him. She must have been in shock and did not know what she was saying. He told me the accident was his fault, that he ran into her car, and he was sorry about that. At this point in the story, whose fault it was really didn't matter, but I listened to him anyway.

I prayed with him, and the look of anguish vanished from his face. When I returned the next day to visit him, I was told by the nurse's station that he passed on to be with Our Lord. I was so relieved his suffering was finally over.

Halloween

Before, during, and after Halloween, I am asked, "Are you a real nun?" A typical costume worn during Halloween is the habit and veil. Our habits and veils are very special to us because it takes a long time—from the time of the calling to making first vows—to don the habit and veil, and to become vessels of the hands and feet of Jesus. The habit and veil are outward signs of the Catholic Faith.

Headstones Face East

Shortly after I finished formation and was shopping in a grocery store, a retired Baptist pastor posed this question to me, "Do you know why all headstones face east?" I *only* wanted to go into the grocery store to buy milk and leave. He explained to me why all the headstones, at least in north Georgia, face east. At that time, I did not know the answer and have learned since, "For as the lightning comes from the east and shines as far as the west, so will be the coming of the Son of man" (Mt. 24:27). Believers hope and trust in the return of Jesus.

Ingles Parking Lot

As I was loading my groceries to the trunk of my car, I noticed a man in an old beat-up car next to me begin to drive off. He stopped, backed up, got out of his car, and approached me. Seeing him walk over to me, I closed the trunk and turned my attention to him. This is how the conversation went:

He said, "Can you help me with a question?"
I said, "Sure."
He said, "I want to hear God. I don't know how to hear him."

I said, "I will tell you what a nun once told me: Light a candle, show up, and shut up. I will say it in a much nicer way though. Light a candle, show up, and be quiet."

He said, "I knew you would know the answer!"

We chatted for a few more minutes about what this means, making the commitment to pray, removing distractions, sitting in the silence, and inviting Jesus into your heart to develop a personal relationship with him. Then I talked about being patient and persevering, and that God's timing is not our timing. He said thank you and drove away.

Inmate in Tijuana Prison Isolation Cell

I met a distraught, young man in the Tijuana Federal Penitentiary who was in an isolation cell of the intellectually challenged area. I learned he loved God so much that he wanted to suffer like Jesus by inflicting pain on himself. He was a cutter. He had been isolated because he was a danger to himself and others. He only spoke in Spanish, and I only spoke English, so I asked a guard to translate for him. After his many tears, and listening to him, I told him that God wants him to be joyful, not sad, and to let God place joy in his heart, and to let go of his sadness. By the time we finished talking and praying together, the Our Father, Hail Mary, and Glory Be prayers (me in English, him in Spanish), he was smiling, not crying. I often wonder where he is today and how he is doing.

Jeep Man

Sister Dolores and I were traveling on Georgia state route 515, and pulled over to a rest stop for a minute so that I could retrieve a couple pieces of dark chocolate from the trunk of the car. While I was digging around in the trunk to look for the food stash, a man who seemed to be about forty years old decided he would check on us to be sure we were okay. What was comical (but dangerous), though, was that he initially drove past us on the main highway, parallel to where we were parked, stopped, *then backed up by driving in reverse into the pull-off ramp, the wrong way, all the way to where we were parked.* We were surprised *he broke the law* just to check on our welfare! I offered him dark chocolate. We told him thank you for checking on us. He drove off into the sunset, never to be seen again. Not by us anyway.

Little Girls at a Department Store

While checking out at the register, a little girl about eight years old was standing close by, and seemed to be waiting for me to finish checking out. We smiled at each other. After I finished checking out, I turned to greet her. This was the conversation:

> Sister: "Hello. How are you?"
> Little girl: "When I grow up, I want to be just like you."
> Sister: "Why would you want to be like me?"
> Little girl: "Because you know Jesus."
> Sister: "Yes, I do know Jesus."

During our very brief conversation, her little sister, about four years old, joined us. I greeted her too. After another short exchange, we all went our separate ways after I said, "God bless you," to both of them. They smiled the entire time we were talking. *This conversation warmed my heart, knowing these little ones already know Jesus.*

Man with a Bloodhound

Once again, Sister Dolores and I were traveling on Georgia state route 515. A man who was driving his car behind us, surprised us. He pulled around my car to drive alongside us, going the same speed I was. He waved. His dog, a bloodhound with long, floppy ears, was slumped over the front car seats, along for the ride with his owner. The dog waved. How? Much to our delight, the driver lifted the paw of the dog, waving his paw for him. Shortly after that, he exited the highway, with both the man and dog waving goodbye. Sister and I still laugh about this memory!

Mental & Spiritual Wellness

At one time, while I was doing Saint Vincent de Paul Society charity work, I prayed with a young man who needed financial assistance. He had mental illness, including schizophrenia. He had also previously attempted suicide several times. He shared these things with me during prayer.

During our discussion, *he asked me if I could help him to be delivered from the evil one.* Well, this is not the type of request we typically receive as Vincentian case workers and prayer warriors, so it surprised me to hear him ask this question. He also desperately wanted to become Catholic. This case quickly became complicated.

According to this man, there were many details about his situation that began when he was a child, and out of respect for his dignity and privacy, I will not provide his name or go into those details.

A couple of books to consider reading are *Possession, Exorcism, and Hauntings,*[97] and *Manual for Spiritual Warfare.*[98]

A person who is trained to assess both mental and spiritual would have been the best person to help this young man. No one at our church had these dual qualifications. Our pastor advised that the individual should first be referred to the bishop for a full evaluation. This means that a mental assessment should first be completed by a certified professional, followed by a spiritual assessment. It is best *not* to assist the person in a spiritual way, until the bishop's office has made a comprehensive assessment.

Murderers

I was having a conversation about prison ministry with a stranger I met in public. He said, "Prison ministry is a waste of time because murderers are going to hell anyway!" Apparently, this person had not read the promises of Jesus Christ in the New Testament. A person with sincere repentance may receive forgiveness for their sins, no matter how grievous the sins are, and still have the promise of heaven.

"...for this is my blood of the covenant, which shall be poured out for many, for the forgiveness of sins" (Mt. 26:28).

Mystical Encounter at Friday Mass

Father Richard Wise celebrated Mass on the Solemnity of the Assumption of Our Blessed Mother into heaven, August 15, 2014. I attended his Mass that day. Here is the email

---

[97] Adam C. Blai, *Possession, Exorcisms, and Hauntings* (Steubenville, Ohio: Emmaus Road Publishing, 2014).
[98] Paul Thigpen, *Manual for Spiritual Warfare* (Charlotte, North Carolina: Tan Books, 2015).

I sent to Father Wise to inform him of what I witnessed during Mass:

"Hello Father,

I wanted to let you know that I saw what appeared to be a host alighting on the walls over you while you celebrated the Eucharistic Liturgy, and also over Our Blessed Mother Mary statue. *At the moment of consecration*, the host "light" descended quickly upon the bread and wine to become the Precious Body and Precious Blood of Jesus. Several times I saw the host alight over Our Blessed Mother Mary and knowing this Mass was being celebrated on the Solemnity of the Assumption of Our Blessed Mother into heaven, and the fact that it was 45 years ago on the day that you became a Priest, I have to believe a divine message was being given to you by Our Lord. I was also greatly moved by how you celebrated that particular Mass compared to other Masses I have seen you do. It was as though you were transfixed with Our Lord and your relationship with him. Thank you so much for all of this Father."

I never witnessed anything like this before. During Mass, I looked around to see if it was possible that the face of someone's watch could have made this reflection on the walls. It was not possible because of the light at that time of day, but especially how this mysterious light moved to specific places over Father and the Blessed Mother.

I learned later that at least one other person, a parishioner of the church, shared with me she saw that the light moved in the exact way I described it. I was relieved someone else saw the same things I did during Mass!

One Day as a Chaplain

After several years of visiting sick patients at the hospital, I came to know which rooms were which, meaning that I knew which rooms were the new mothers with babies, which rooms had actively dying patients, and which ones were knee replacements and severe diverticulitis cases.

I visited an actively-dying man with his wife by his side every day for a week. I honestly believe I ministered to her more than him, because she was very distraught. He slept most of the time, so I did not get to speak with him very often.

At the end of that week, I arrived at the hospital to find that he had passed away, and this was so sad to me, because his wife was very upset about losing him. I walked to the other end of the hall, to see a new baby in its mother's arms. God orchestrated my day that way. He had me experience death first, birth second. I was grateful I was able to see new life at the end of my work week.

Pilgrimage to Rome

Just before starting my formation with the Eudist Servants of the Eleventh Hour, I went on a pilgrimage to Rome, Italy. I was visiting my oldest son, Chris, a U.S. Air Force pilot stationed at Ramstein Air Base, Germany. He asked me if I wanted to travel somewhere in Europe. I said that I had never been to the Vatican and would love to go. So, we did. We only had a couple of days in Rome, during March 2-5, 2012, but we had a lovely time.

We saw many of the famous places in Rome. The artwork of the Vatican's Sistine Chapel was inspiring to me, especially Michelangelo's famous frescoes. This is also the room where the College of Cardinals gather to vote for a new Pope.

Another place in Rome that greatly impacted me was personally experiencing the "Scala Sancta" (translated - the Sacred Steps). Catholic News Agency captures the description of these steps as:

> "The bare, white marble of Rome's 'Scala Sancta,' which are believed to be the stairs trod by Christ on the day of his trial and death, are exposed and visible to pilgrims for the first time in almost 300 years. The Holy Stairs are held to be those which led to the praetorium of Pontius Pilate in Jerusalem, and which Christ would have ascended on his way to the trial before his Crucifixion. According to tradition, the stairs were brought to Rome by Saint Helena in the 4th century. The mother of Constantine the Great, it is believed that she restored many sites in the Holy Land and discovered the True Cross, in addition to other relics. The stairs, which are near the Archbasilica of Saint John Lateran, were first opened to the public more than 400 years ago by Sixtus V. Pilgrims who visit the stairs must ascend them on their knees as a sign of piety and reverence but can choose how they wish to pray while doing so. Those who cannot climb on their knees may kneel on the first step and then walk up one of the other staircases to reach the top. There is also a plenary indulgence, or the remittance of temporal punishment due to sins which have already been forgiven, attached to ascending the entire staircase."[99]

Climbing the steps on my knees is a special memory, thinking of Jesus in his passion before the crucifixion, being drawn closer to him with each step. It is believed these are the steps Jesus walked to his death. This was also an exercise

---

[99] Hannah Brockhaus, "Rome's 'Holy Stairs' uncovered for the first time in 300 years," *Catholic News Agency*, April 11, 2019.

of offering the pain and agony of my knees and back for those people I knew who were lost and suffering.

Power of Prayer

This is a story about the father of my children, my ex-husband, Dean. In the fall of 2011, he was hospitalized with sepsis, several months before I entered formation to become a Catholic sister. The following is from an email I still have, dated December 10, 2011, emailed to him at 12:26 pm:

> "Welcome back to the land of the living! You have had a difficult time and many have been praying for your full recovery. I am in four different prayer groups and since the time you entered the hospital, we have all been praying for you. Many complete strangers have been praying for you to make it through all of this, gain strength one day at a time, and survive the infection. We are so very glad to see you are well on our way to getting back to a normal life. At one point I sent an email on November 16th to all of the family asking them to pray the Divine Mercy Chaplet for you at 7:30 p.m. one evening. This means that everyone who read the email, and chose to pray for you and to give you strength through this difficult time, prayed with me, for your sake. *Within 24–48 hours after this, two of our sons were telling me that the nursing staff began to pull the tubes out of you, one-by-one.* This is a true story. I do not always understand the mystery of what God does and why, but the more I move in this direction (towards God), the more I "see" and understand. Good always comes from what we perceive to be bad."

When I reflect on this email, I remember talking with him on the phone, sharing something I learned from the sisters about people who are spared death. The explanation I learned, which makes sense to me, and I shared with him, was that there must be something God wanted him to do in life, some reason God wanted him to stay with us. It was not his time to go.

This became even more evident when he told me there were five other people in the Infectious Diseases unit who had sepsis, and they all died, *except him.*

Additionally, the mother of a woman who worked in my old office that I retired from, was hospitalized at the same time he was, with sepsis and also a diabetic. Both were dealing with similar afflictions at the same time. God chose to take her to heaven. She was a good and loving person who believed in God and went to church regularly to give him praise and thanksgiving. God must have had something more for Dean to do, to leave him on this earth, at least until he passed away several years later. God was merciful to the father of my sons, for some reason, at that time.

Precious Blood Daily Devotional

On November 4, 2011, I received a call from a friend, Mary Bernadette, a very spiritual, Catholic woman. She was formerly of the Buddhist faith, but had converted to Catholicism. She is deceased now, but I believe she was the most prayerful woman I have ever met. She shared that she would begin prayer at 3:00 a.m. every morning, and end at 11:00 a.m. She said she would see the Gospels of the Bible play out in front of her while she prayed. And she said she bled from her temple area when she prayed ardently. I never saw her bleed while she was praying, but I also did not have any reason *not* to believe her.

She and I shared an experience that evening, an unexplained mystical event.

She called me at 7:15 p.m. while I was eating dinner. We chatted for a few minutes, and then we said goodbye. A few minutes passed, and she called me again. This time she was distraught. Within those few minutes, she saw a picture of the bloodied Jesus Christ appear next to my name in her list of phone contacts after we hung up the first time. She wanted to know how and why this happened. She called me the second time to ask me to explain.

She wanted me to explain what happened to her phone. She spoke in broken English-Vietnamese language and it was difficult to understand what she was so upset about. I told her that I would come to her house after I finished dinner.

When I arrived at her house, she handed me her phone and asked me to explain what happened. She was talking about her altars too. I saw one altar in the living room area. Then she showed me the second altar in her bedroom.

There was a connection of some kind between her phone and the altar. Still not understanding what the problem was, except that it was something about my name in her phone, I scrolled through her contacts list.

A little background about her is that she was eighty years old when this happened, she did not own a computer, and her phone was only a month old. She was *not* technologically-gifted.

As I was standing in her bedroom, I looked at her contacts list and saw there were fifty-eight contacts in her phone. Names were listed. All contacts had the gray profile image. There were no pictures, except one. *Only one contact had a picture next to it. It was my name.* She had typed it in as "Patsystleos Power." Patsy was my family nickname. "Stleos" was an abbreviation of the name of the Catholic Church I belonged to at that time.

I saw the picture next to my name in her phone. The picture was the face of the bloodied Jesus Christ.

Then something told me to look over at her altar. Remember that when I say "something," it is my belief that it is Jesus himself speaking to me.

She had about fifty items on her altar. My eye immediately went to the cover page of the *Precious Blood of Jesus Daily Devotional* book.[100] The picture on the phone next to my name was the exact picture on the front of this devotional book!

Seeing this, I became breathless. I could hardly breathe to see this, *knowing* there was no way for her to generate this picture herself, to insert his picture next to my name in her phone, *within those few minutes in between the two phone calls earlier that evening.*

She said that when she called me the first time, the picture was not there. I asked her about this, and she said it was not there. *After she spoke with me on the first phone call, the picture suddenly appeared on her phone next to my name, which is why she called me immediately to ask why this happened. Well, at that time, I had no idea of why or how it happened.*

I told her that I would come back Sunday afternoon to take a picture of her phone and her daily devotional book. The photo that I added to this book for the reader shows a picture of her phone next to the front page of the devotional book.

---

[100] The Adorers of the Precious Blood, *Precious Blood of Jesus Daily Devotional* (Tallahassee, Florida: Association of the Precious Blood, 2007). To learn more, visit: *www.PreciousBloodInternational.com.*

Precious Blood of Jesus Daily Devotional next to
Mary Bernadette's cell phone - 2011

I believe that this unexplained, mystical event is yet another confirmation from Jesus that I am to serve the least of his brothers and sisters. I also believe he wants me to pray this devotional, which requires a significant commitment of prayer that lasts for many months, and would be in addition to my existing prayer regimen.

Prayer is more powerful than anything else we can do.

After this event happened, I asked a person who I respected as a devout practicing Christian, Reese, what he thought of the devotional book, which I showed to him. He looked at the Table of Contents and said that I am being prepared to be ordained. I told him that I could not be ordained in the Catholic Church, *but that I could become consecrated to Jesus.* This was another confirmation that I was going in the right direction, as it was consistent with the calling to become a consecrated sister.

I spent some quiet time reflecting on this unexplained event afterward. I noticed the following on page two of the devotional book: "Please contact us with details about all miracles, large and small, or any unusual phenomenon associated with this devotion."

God has such a sense of humor.

I shared this experience with my sons. One of them suggested it might be easy for my friend to snap a picture of the front of the devotional book and save it to my name in the list of contacts on the phone. Of course, that could be done; however, if one looks at the photo carefully, they will see the picture fits into the gray place holder perfectly, corner-to-corner. And the owner of the phone was a woman who was not technologically-gifted to do this. She certainly could not have done this in a few minutes, during the time between the first call and the second call. Also, no one was living with her who could have made this happen. And why would anyone do this anyway, is the bigger question? And why only my name, no one else?

An additional note about her is that she recorded her unpublished testimony, dated December 17, 2007. She shared it with me, which is in a small booklet format. She asked that I help her spread the news about this *Precious Blood of Jesus Daily Devotional.*[101] Here is an excerpt from her written testimony:

> "Throughout the years, I keep praying to God and asking Him if there would be anything that He would have me to do for Him. In June 2007, as I closed my eyes during prayer, Jesus spoke to my heart. He instructed me to go to a church to search for a book and proceeded to describe the front cover of the book. He said that the book would have a face that is pierced with twisted metal thorns and stained with blood. He also said to me, 'My dear, you can

---

[101] The Adorers of the Precious Blood, *Precious Blood of Jesus Daily Devotional* (Tallahassee, Florida: Association of the Precious Blood, 2007). To learn more, visit: *www.PreciousBloodInternational.com.*

no longer pray for your own sake. You need to spread the devotion [throughout] the whole world.' I shared the inspiration with my friend, Ninh, who later spotted a similar book described by Jesus through my prayers. As Ninh exited the church after the daily Mass, a book fell from the pile of books that a person was carrying. The book landed right in front of her. She noticed that the cover was similar to what I had described to her. Ninh borrowed the book for me. The book was entitled *Precious Blood of Jesus Daily Devotional*, and was published by the Adorers of the Precious Blood... I do not have any exact plan on how to spread the devotion or to distribute the devotional book, but I will keep on praying. Once again, I trust that God will lead me one step at a time and leave everything in God's hands."

She was not able to spread the news about this devotional before she died. She was going blind and had difficulty even going to daily Mass. Hopefully, with the publishing of *this* book, people will become familiar with this *Precious Blood of Jesus Daily Devotional*[102] book, and incorporate it into their lives. There is no question Jesus is dropping not-so-subtle hints to do so.

Seeking the Truth

At a detention center, we started a new prison ministry program with a team from a local Catholic Church. After teaching a class for almost two hours, a man came up to us afterward to say he thought he wanted to be baptized as a Catholic. I asked him why he would like to do this. He said,

---

[102] The Adorers of the Precious Blood, *Precious Blood of Jesus Daily Devotional* (Tallahassee, Florida: Association of the Precious Blood, 2007). To learn more, visit: *www.PreciousBloodInternational.com.*

"Because now I know this is the truth." He was seeking. We set up a meeting between him and the priest to begin discussions, and gave him the *YOUCAT Catechism*[103] book to study. We followed up with him every week to discuss his studies.

Solar Eclipse Pictures

On August 21, 2017, a solar eclipse took place that many people were able to witness in the United States. From where I lived at the time, in the north Georgia mountains, I was able to clearly see the eclipse. A candidate who happened to be a medical doctor, was living with me, preparing to become a Catholic sister with our association of sisters. She and I set up our lawn chairs in the driveway, and we donned our special protective sunglasses that were made specifically for these types of events. As the eclipse began, we noticed how the temperature was dropping, that it was much cooler outside. We also noticed a fragrance in the air that was unusual.

At the moment when the sun became fully eclipsed by the moon, over my house, something told me to take pictures. Whenever I say "something told me," it is usually the Holy Spirit/Jesus telling me what to do. **I took five pictures, then I heard, "That is enough."** Immediately after the eclipse, I looked at the pictures, then showed them to the candidate.

When I saw the pictures, I thought I was seeing things. I showed them to the candidate immediately after I saw them, and she had the same thoughts I did. There is what appears to be a nucleus of some sort in the center of the eclipsed sun. How could this be?

---

[103] Christoph von Schönborn, *YOUCAT: Youth Catechism of the Catholic Church* (San Francisco: Ignatius Press, 2011).

This event will be more understandable when looking at the photos. The original photos were not edited, except to enlarge them so you can better see the center. The pictures are in successive order.

I took these pictures when the sun was totally eclipsed, when what we saw with our eyes was black, not white like the pictures below, which is also curious.

The first of the five pictures, is a white circle, followed by the same picture, cropped, and the last picture is a magnification of the center of the picture, to allow you to better see the center. In these photos, there is nothing in the center. All three of these pictures are the first picture I took of the eclipse.

<u>The second of the five pictures</u>, is also a white circle, followed by the same picture, cropped, and the last picture is a magnification of the center of the picture. Again, there is nothing in the center of these photos. <u>All three of these photos are the second picture I took of the eclipse.</u>

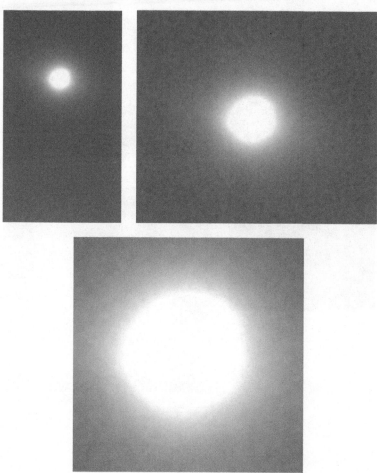

The third of the five pictures, shows a gray circle within the white circle, which looks like a "nucleus of cells," followed by the same picture, cropped, and the last picture is a magnified photo[104] of the center of the picture. All three of these photos are the third picture I took of the eclipse.

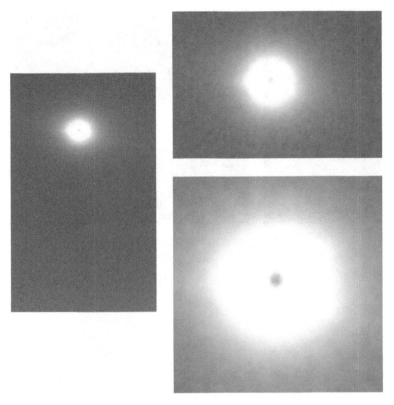

---

[104] In the third picture, the brightness and contrast were increased to better show the center of the photo.

The fourth of five pictures, shows a collection of pieces within the "nucleus" that have formed together into an "X," no longer individual sections, and followed by the same picture, cropped. Included here is also the magnified photo[105] of the center of the picture. All three of these photos are the fourth picture I took of the eclipse.

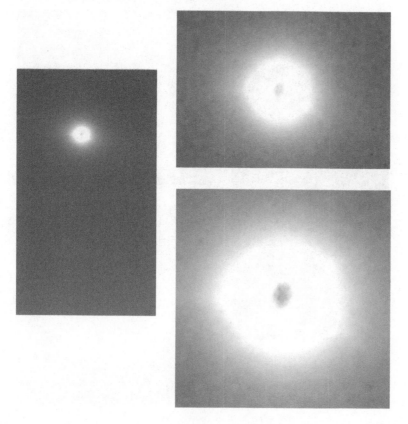

---

[105] In the third picture, the brightness and contrast were increased to better show the center of the photo.

The fifth and last picture shows a collection of pieces still joined together within the "nucleus," no longer individual parts, and appears interestingly enough, to be in the form of an unborn baby. The third picture is the magnified photo[106] of the center of the picture. All three of these photos are the fifth picture I took of the eclipse.

<hr />

[106] In the third picture, the brightness and contrast were increased to better show the center of the photo.

The candidate then shared with me, after she saw the pictures, that she was carrying guilt from observing an abortion during her medical internship. She felt guilty for what happened, even though she did not perform, or participate in, the act of abortion.

She did not want to participate in any way in the abortion procedure because of her Catholic faith. She believed in the dignity of life of the baby. *She was told she would have to observe the procedure anyway.* She was allowed to speak with the patient before the procedure. Then the abortion was performed.

I informed the candidate she should meet with one of our priests to discuss the anguish she was still carrying. The priest she met with, Father Wise, shared with her that while he worked on death row as a Catholic Chaplain in the late 1980s, he had to witness a man being put to death under the death penalty. This was at a time when the electric chair was used to execute a prisoner in Georgia. Now the method of execution is by lethal injection.

The priest and the candidate learned they had something in common. They both witnessed murder, even though they did not support these practices, and did not want to see them carried out. Killing a prisoner and killing a baby are both pro-life issues.

Prisoners are already serving their sentences by losing their liberties. They are paying for their crimes while serving time in prison. When we execute prisoners, we interrupt the work God is doing with their souls. There have been many conversions of men and women that have taken place in prisons, because the light of Christ can live within them, even while they are incarcerated.

And we need to always pray for victims of heinous crimes, and their families, who experience the loss of their family members in tragic ways. Pray that they may be consoled in the loss of their loved ones. Pray that there may be peace among everyone involved. I have the deepest admiration for people who can sincerely forgive those who have hurt their family members. Our family members mean so much to us.

The candidate and I agreed that her coming to stay with me for a month to prepare to become a sister was about her finally learning how to process the anguish she carried for years from observing the abortion.

She and I also agreed that through the pictures that were taken that day, God wanted to let her know the baby was fine, and in heaven with him. She was very relieved to know this.

We would learn shortly after this event that her journey was not about becoming a sister, because she soon chose to marry. This sometimes happens during the discernment part of the journey.

Spirit in Billeting

My mother and I traveled to attend my brother's wedding. This was before I received the calling to become a sister. We stayed in billeting at an Air Force Base. Taps played at 10:00 p.m. to signal lights out on the base. As soon as taps started, simultaneously, water began running in the shower of our room. I did not get up; neither did my mother. The water ran until the end of taps, stopping *exactly* when it ended. The water only ran at *exactly* the beginning and end of taps. That was curious, but what was strange was that both my mother and I were in bed when this happened. We were not in the bathroom when taps played.

Curious, I got out of bed and walked toward the bathroom, then became afraid of what I might find. I asked my mother to go into the bathroom with me. She was getting upset with me because she wanted to go to sleep, and she said she did not believe that restless spirits existed. She said, "Oh land!"

This was one of our mother's statements she would make when she was frustrated. She reluctantly got out of bed and came over to lock arms with me as we courageously walked into the bathroom. I pulled back the shower curtain to see that the shower walls were completely wet!

So, who turned the water on and off in our room during taps?

Neither of us had taken a shower that night. We always took our showers in the morning. Realizing the showers were not turned on and off by either one of us that night, I became anxious and breathless. There was no *reasonable* explanation for this.

At the billeting office, checking out the next morning, I happened to tell the clerk how strange it was the night before, staying in our room. The supervisor heard me talking about taps and the water running at exactly the same time, and the wet shower walls. She said, "Years ago before the barracks you are staying in was renovated, there was a mother who died in the bathtub in the room you stayed in last night. The child is supposedly still looking for her mother, and also rides a red tricycle."

We flew back to Atlanta and spent the night in my apartment. I was relieved we were no longer in that billeting room. That night though, as we began to fall asleep, we heard a scrambling sound on the bathroom vanity counter top, right next to my bedroom. It sounded like someone was moving items around on the counter top. I heard it and said nothing. She heard the scrambling noise and said, "What the heck is that?!" I said, "I don't know. Let's go to sleep." The next morning, I was the first to get up, and I went into the bathroom to find *absolutely nothing was out of place* on the counter top. Again, there was no explanation for this. It is the only time that ever happened in my apartment.

We traveled back to Warner Robins, Georgia, where Mom lived at the time. The incidents ended with the travel, as far as I know.

Saint Vincent de Paul Society Client

On June 20, 2014, I met a Saint Vincent de Paul Society client. He said fourteen KKK members assaulted him in 2009. He was in a wheelchair as a result of the beatings. His doctor told him that he would never walk again. He had a very positive outlook on life and was spiritually grounded. *He exuded the light of Christ simply with his presence. He now writes love poems to God.* After praying with him, he asked if I wanted to hear one of his poems. He had memorized it. He recited a very long and touching poem to me. I cried. The case worker took care of his needs. This man and I wished each other well and said goodbye. His story broke my heart.

Saint Vincent de Paul Society Conference – Friendship

As the conference level spiritual advisor, I facilitated a two-hour meeting with several Vincentians about a significant issue regarding a lack of friendship among themselves. Friendship is one of the essential elements[107] of the Saint Vincent de Paul Society. During our Vincentian meetings and when we serve the poor, we cultivate our Vincentian friendships with one another. *We prayed before we began this*

---

[107] *Manual of the Society of St. Vincent de Paul in the United States*, National Council of the United States, Society of St. Vincent de Paul, Inc., 2019, Chapter 3, Section 3.1, Essential Elements, pg. 50.

two-hour meeting, and I am sure this is the very reason our meeting was productive.

The Ruler and The Knuckles

The following is a typical exchange I have with older gentlemen who approach me in public to say, "Sister, I want to tell you about Sister *(fill in the blank)* of order *(fill in the blank)* who used a ruler on my knuckles. She was tough!" It is always a man who approaches me in this way, and he insists on showing me his knuckles.

This opening exchange has taken place in many grocery stores, gas stations, and other public places. The conversation typically begins with men in their seventies who are compelled to share how hard it was for them to be educated by a Catholic nun. My response is, "I am so sorry that happened to you (and I *am* sorry), but look how well you turned out!" We both smile and go on our merry ways.

Wearing a Turban

The air conditioning was not working in my dentist's office. After I had my teeth cleaned, I went to the front desk to pay my bill. While I waited my turn, another patient was complaining about how hot it was, then pointed to me, saying, "And look at her! She is wearing a turban on her head! She *must* be hot!" To be clear, we wear a cap and veil on our heads. Not a turban. They are part of our attire.

Questions for the reader to contemplate: What stories might you have on your journey? Do you wonder? Have you already had events like this happen to you? What else do you think God might have in store for you?

CHAPTER 13
NEW VOCATIONS AND AN INVITATION

—✦—

The night before I wrote this chapter, I talked with Jesus, as I did before every chapter I wrote for this book, asking him to help me write it. I spent two days with writer's block, with no clue of how to make this particular chapter come together.

All the other chapters before this were also a struggle, trying to understand the Table of Contents that Jesus gave me to write about. I was wrestling with this chapter much more than the others though.

Like all the other chapters, I already had the resources I collected over the previous ten years, e.g., saints' prayers, prose, books, daily devotionals, and journal writings, to collate into something that made sense.

Then the focus of this chapter changed unexpectedly. Before I address what happened to change the focus of this chapter, I would like to share the following useful information regarding vocations, because one of the themes of this book is about increasing religious vocations.

Information on religious vocations is available at *www.vocationnetwork.org* and *www.usccb.org*. These are just a few places a person can review for more information. Dioceses may also hold vocation discernment retreats. Contact the Office of Vocations within your diocese for more information. Sometimes the diocese will also provide vocations newsletters to those who are discerning a religious vocation.

Additionally, the National Vocation Awareness Week takes place every year for men and women discerning religious vocations.

Also, the Apostolic Exhortation on the *Call to Holiness in Today's World*, of Pope Francis, guides us to learn more about being called in these times. It is a short resource of eighty-eight pages.[108]

A couple of inspiring quotes from his book that resonated with me are:

- We are called "Each in his or her own way..." (pg. 12)

- "God's life is communicated 'to some in one way and to others in another.'" (pg. 13)

- "This should excite and encourage us to give our all and embrace that unique plan God willed for each of us from eternity: 'Before I formed you in the womb, I knew you, and before you were born, I consecrated you.'" (Jer 1:5) (pg. 13)

After conversations with Jesus that I had the night before writing this chapter, and the morning of writing this chapter, in prayer, I pushed aside almost everything I thought I was to write about for this chapter. *The focus is still on new vocations and an invitation to serve; however, now I know why he is asking for more vocations.*

The conversations with Jesus changed everything for this chapter.

---

[108] Pope Francis, *Gaudete et exsultate*, April 9, 2018. *www.vatican.va/ content/francesco/en/apost_exhortations/documents/papa-francesco_esortazione-ap_20180319_gaudete-et-exsultate.html.*

Usually, Jesus speaks to me as soon as I wake up, while I am in the silence. During the night was a unique experience, because he and I talked most of the night, while at the same time, I tried to sleep. I was restless all night long. *Nothing made sense to me in our discussions, until the morning of writing this chapter.*

Jesus said, "It's about the babies."
I said, "The babies?"
He said, "This is *why* I need more vocations. You are still killing babies, committing sins of the flesh, and polluting the earth. These are all *my* creations. I need many more priests, deacons, brothers, and sisters *to help others understand HOW to change.*"

What is the title of this book's first chapter? *You Are Who You Aren't.* From the time he gave me this title in 1998, over twenty years ago, I knew this book would be about changes people go through in life, but that was all I knew at the time.

This must be the reason he wanted me to write a spiritual autobiography of what happens when one middle-aged woman says "yes" to the calling, making drastic changes to become who God has been waiting for, then using her to do his work to serve those who suffer.

Hopefully, this book has given single men and women a glimpse of the journey one person can have when called to serve others for God, as an ordained priest or deacon, or consecrated brother or sister. When I say single, I mean, (1) a person who has never been married, 2) a person who is divorced with an annulment, or (3) a widow/widower.

All Catholic orders, congregations, and associations have their specific formation processes that require the candidate to grow in humility, obedience, poverty, chastity, and unconditional love for others. These organizations differ in their charisms, formation, vows, and service.

A person who has been called, must seek answers to their questions until they find where they are supposed to be. It is not an overnight process. A seeker must research the organizations, discern with prayer, go to Eucharistic Adoration to pray, speak with spiritual directors, priests, deacons, brothers or sisters, and take other actions, as necessary.

A person must discern, in prayer, to discover which path to take. It is different for everyone. Not everyone will have unexplained mystical events, or hear the Holy Spirit speak to them, for example. This does not necessarily mean they do not have a calling to serve the suffering Christ either. What is ideal is to have clergy or a spiritual director to turn to with your questions.

Jesus invites us to journey towards our vocations. He waits for everyone to follow the calling of the vocation that God grants to each person. If God calls you to be a mother, be the best mother you can be. If he calls you to be a father, be the best father you can be. If he calls you to be a consecrated brother, and you have discerned this to be true, then follow the calling to become the best consecrated brother you can be.

When I was much younger, I entered the vocation of a married spouse and active-duty Air Force airman. After this, I became a Veteran, mother, grandmother and career businesswoman, which are all their own individual types of vocations. Finally, I became a Catholic sister, a vocation I never asked for. Now I am grateful to God for this.

Welcome Jesus into your heart. Welcome him with a genuine yearning to get to know him on a personal level. What do you have to lose? Give it a try, but if you do, really mean it, that you are sincere about inviting him into your heart, to be your best friend. He will be with you in the darkest and loneliest times of your life. He has been there for me in many situations.

Trust him. Know that he is there for you also. Know that he is with you, whether you spend time with him or not, and as you go through the difficult times in life.

Tragically, many people die alone and without family members around them. I pray they have a strong faith to accompany them through their extreme pain. And I pray for those who do not have faith strong enough to carry them through.

I am especially grateful to know there are spiritually-grounded medical staff who are willing to pray with patients. My sister, Jackie, in her sacred calling as a nurse, is one of those prayer warriors. Her patients are fortunate to have her, and all those who have sacred callings to serve the suffering Christ.

All that a person needs is faith as small as a mustard seed. If you place a mustard seed in the palm of your hand, you can see just how little it is. Just a tiny bit of faith is what Jesus said we need to get started[109]

A bit of humor to go with this chapter is that my television remote became defective the day before writing this chapter, which was also the day before the Holy Triduum[110] began. I could turn on the television, but I could not change channels. I only had one channel. However, I could still watch the events of Holy Week and Easter from my laptop.

God has such a sense of humor. He removed the opportunity to watch anything on television on the day before the beginning of the Holy Triduum to make sure I

---

[109] Mt. 17:20.

[110] "The Easter Triduum begins with the evening Mass of the Lord's Supper on Holy Thursday, reaches its high point in the Easter Vigil, and closes with Evening Prayer on Easter Sunday." (U.S. Catholic Council of Bishops, "Eighteen Questions on the Paschal Triduum." *www.usccb.org/prayer-and-worship/liturgical-year-and-calendar/triduum/questions-and-answers*).

would finish writing this chapter that day. Jesus told me that morning that I would write this chapter in one day. And so, I did.

This explains why I had a headache, sleep deprivation, and was overwhelmed by what Jesus was instructing me to write about, and how he was connecting everything in the book, to reveal to me.

This morning he told me *why* I need to write about the need for more vocations.

Me: "Why do I need to write about needing more [religious] vocations?"
Jesus: "The reason is that we need more religious leaders to fight evil."
Me: "What evil are you referring to, because there are so many different types of evil in the world today?"
Jesus: "Killing your own unborn babies."

He was not specifically referencing me having abortions, because I have never had an abortion; he was talking about the fact that, as a nation, we are still killing our own children. If you remember, two earlier chapters ended with reference to "baby." It has been curious to me why those chapters ended that way. *Remember, Jesus guided me through the writing of this book. I did not know why those chapters ended concerning babies, until now.*

Until I began writing this chapter, I did not realize all the times "baby" was referenced in this book:

Chapter 1 – How we change as we are developing in the womb, as babies.
Chapter 4 – The chapter ends concerning a long-awaited messiah, a baby, Jesus Christ.
Chapter 8 – A soul accompanies a newly-created baby.
Chapter 9 – The chapter ends with "A baby."

Chapter 12 – Story of meeting with an inmate whose eleven-week-old baby died of SIDs.

Chapter 12 – Story of pictures of a solar eclipse, containing what appeared to be a baby in the center of one the photos.

Chapter 12 – Story of visiting a family in the hospital with a new baby.

And the vision that I received from the Holy Spirit, of this book's front cover, includes an expectant mother.

Now it all makes sense.

This book has become not only what one religious vocation journey looks like, but it is also to discuss WHY Jesus is calling for more journeys like this, and to help those who are called with their conversions of heart, mind, and soul, to move beyond who they are, to become who God has been waiting for.

The timing of the writing of this book could not be more perfect. I wrote the first draft of this book within the first couple months of sheltering-in-place, due to COVID-19.

The impact of COVID-19 has slowed down single people to a place of complete, controlled silence. Single people without dependents are the ones God needs for religious vocations to become priests and consecrated brothers and sisters, specifically. This does not discount the fact that he also needs lay people. These vocations are just as important as religious vocations. And although most deacons are married, together they and their wives greatly contribute to the ministries of the church, especially in the administering of the Sacraments of the church. *All vocations matter.*

People who have read about the history of the church, have seen that since the time Jesus walked this earth over 2,000 years ago, there have always been people chosen by God to continue to lead people spiritually, to administer the

Sacraments, and to console those who suffer. *Our time is no different.*

I especially like the following quote as it is a true statement of the opportunity of what life offers to us: "You can't go back and change the beginning but you can start where you are and change the ending."[111]

If you choose to be a soldier of God, a servant, and the hands and feet of Jesus, trust God that, "Blessed are you who believed that what was spoken to you by the Lord would be fulfilled" (Lk. 1:45).

God will give you all the grace you need to fulfill what he asks of you. He will open doors that need to be opened, he will place the people you need around you, and he will do all of this in his perfect timing.

The Holy Spirit reminded me of two famous people who gave validity to what he was asking me to write, i.e., that it is imperative more people answer the calling to religious life, to battle for the respect and dignity of all life, from conception to natural death.

The first person, Saint Teresa of Calcutta, formerly Mother Teresa, told us: "Any country that accepts abortion is not teaching its people love, but to use violence to get what they want. This is why the greatest destroyer of love is abortion."[112]

The second person, Saint [Pope] John Paul II, said, "Respect for life requires that science and technology should always be at the service of man and his integral development. Society as a whole must respect, defend, and promote the

---

[111] Originally thought to be a quote of C.S. Lewis; however, in researching this quote, this may not be true.
[112] "Clinton, Mother Teresa, and All Those Babies," *Washington Examiner.* September 4, 2016.

dignity of every human person, at every moment and in every condition of that person's life."[113]

How we treat people speaks volumes of who we are in our civility as a country. This includes born and unborn children, incarcerated, immigrants, drug addicts, intellectually challenged, and all of the marginalized.

Once we decide to accept a religious vocation, our search for answers does not end. The *Little Blue Book* states, "A relationship with Jesus is so rich and so full that it requires a lifetime to discover all of its meaning and beauty. To think that I could appreciate everything about my faith in less than a lifetime would be like tourists who think they could see all of Europe in eight days."[114]

The journey of my vocation continues...

In January of 2018, Jesus flooded me with stuff again. He said, "It's time to go out again. It's time to live closer to family because you are getting older. It's time to do death row prison ministry. *It's time to write the book.*" This was a lot to discern all at one time. Discernment takes time and patience, done correctly.

Of course, I could not do all these things at the same time. Once I took my time to fully discern these things, I first informed my superior and the diocese that I was going to relocate to live closer to family, because I was getting older, approaching sixty-five years old. I thought it would be wise to relocate while I was still physically able to, rather than to wait until I was older, when the task would be much more difficult.

---

[113] Saint John Paul II, *Evangelium Vitae*, March 25, 1995.

[114] *Little Books of the Diocese of Saginaw, Inc: Advent/Christmas Season: Little Blue Book 2019*, based on the writings of Bishop Ken Untener (Saginaw, Diocese of Saginaw Inc., 2019).

I was moving within the same diocese, so a letter from my superior to the bishop was not needed; however, I informed my superior and diocese of my new address.

After I got settled at the new location, and after approvals were given, I continued doing prison ministry. I began working at the Metro Transitional Center, Gwinnett County Detention Center, and visiting one death row inmate at the Georgia Diagnostic and Classification Prison in Jackson, Georgia.[115] I am thankful to Deacon Richard Tolcher and Father Adam Ozimek for helping me get re-established in prison ministry after I relocated.

I have also done prison ministry at the Atlanta Federal Penitentiary, Phillips Prison, and visited inmates at Walker State Prison,[116] all located in Georgia.

Our Georgia Catholics Against the Death Penalty[117] team that I am part of, continues to work with the Atlanta Archdiocese and other religious, private, and state organizations, under the leadership of Deacon Erik Wilkinson, with the mission of educating others on the facts of why the death penalty should be abolished.[118]

Although the number of people on death row in Georgia is fewer, this penalty is still a legal option for juries to choose. It should be eliminated for many reasons, and most especially because a civil society respects life from conception to natural

---

[115] Then later I was given permission by the Chief of Chaplains in January, 2022, to begin working as a volunteer in G-block, which houses the death row inmates. As of October, 2022, there are 37 Georgia death row inmates, of which five Catholic prisoners receive the Eucharist during my chaplain visits.

[116] This is a Georgia faith-based and character-based prison. Inmates at other Georgia prisons can submit an application to be considered for a transfer to this prison. For more information, look up Walker State Prison at *www.gdc.ga.gov* for a summary of their programs.

[117] For more information about this organization, visit *www.gacadp.org*.

[118] To learn more about the facts and reasons to end the death penalty, go to the Death Penalty Information Center (DPIC) website, *www.deathpenaltyinfo.org*.

death. We are all divine creations of God, even after heinous crimes are committed. God doesn't measure sin/crimes. *He forgives everyone regardless of how bad their sins are, as long as they are truly sorry, and ask for forgiveness from him.*

This is a pro-life issue.

I would be remiss if I did not highlight that when the death penalty is carried out, this interferes with the good work God is doing with a prisoner's soul. It can take years to grow in faith, and to become repentant about one's own crimes/sins. When this growth is interrupted by an execution of death, hope for repentance is lost.

And to repeat the important words written earlier in chapter 11 of this book, "Please always pray for victims of crime (especially heinous crime) and their families. Unless we have been in the shoes of a family member of a victim, who has lost them to a heinous crime, we will never comprehend the depth of their loss. But one thing we can do for the families is to pray for them. Pray that they will be consoled in the loss of their loved ones, taken much too soon from this life. *It is difficult to understand why God would allow heinous crimes to happen to his own creations. I hope he will tell us when we get to heaven.* In the meantime, pray for the victims and their families, the prisoners and their families, for forgiveness of those who committed heinous crimes, and peace for everyone involved."

Our collective prayers will make a difference, because prayer petitions to God are more powerful than anything else we could do anyway.

To close this chapter, and ending with my current role as the St. Vincent de Paul Society-Georgia Council spiritual advisor, and chairman of the spirituality committee, I have the opportunity to educate Vincentians on the importance of deepening their spiritually, and praying with those they serve, who are the marginalized people of our society. It is through this prayerful service that we grow in our own faith.

> *Questions for the reader to contemplate: What will I do? Will I become a true, faith-filled spiritual leader, working to perpetuate good works, in order to renew our society in a spiritual way?*

CHAPTER 14
QUESTIONS FOR BABY BOOMERS

‒⁄⁀‿

Spiritually, our country is dying, and has been for some time.

We continue to hear of drug overdoses, abortions, starving children, human trafficking, and sex trafficking, just to name a few.

We no longer respect life, and the dignity of a person? I want to believe our country respects life of *every* human being.

Maybe we have gotten used to the injustices? Have we become numb, thinking we can do nothing about these evil acts against humanity? Clearly, these crimes against humanity are overwhelming for one person to fix. It will take the involvement of many people to make a significant impact.

Do we care about the dignity of life? I think we do.

The "baby boomer" generation is a *massive workforce of [mostly] retirees* in our country today. Many no longer draw a paycheck; however, millions of retired citizens have a pension, social security income, and are financially self-sufficient. I am part of this workforce.

Workforce, because *our generation can choose to work, even after retirement, to help this country.* We have time, talent, and treasure to offer to an ailing nation.

Pure joy is found in helping others. People need our help, expertise and knowledge. In my view, this is the purpose of our lives, to help those in need.

After retiring from our demanding jobs, and after we enjoy a temporary sabbatical of peace and readjustment to our lives after retirement, will we choose to help our country?

Many of us have children and grandchildren. Some baby boomers question if they can commit to give of themselves, because they are already committed to caring for their families. *Striking a balance between family and volunteerism can be done.*

Our children are grown with their own families. They will let us know when they need help, and if we can help them, we will. Our bonds with our children are never broken.

"For we are his workmanship, created in Christ Jesus for good works, which God prepared beforehand, that we should walk in them" (Eph. 2:10). Prepared beforehand means God had a plan for us before we were conceived. Inconceivable by our simple human minds to even contemplate how this could be, but it is true if we believe the sacred scriptures of the Holy Bible.

The question still remains though, what is God's will for me in my later years of life?

Ask God, in prayer, to reveal to you what he wants you to do. Eventually, he will tell you, or show you, what he wants of you. He will do this in his timing, not our timing, and if it is in accordance with his will for you. Trust that he will give you what you need along the way. What he asks of you might be simple and easy, taking a little of your time. He will not ask you to move a mountain!

As older folks, we also consider the limitations of health. As we age, our physiological systems break down. Sometimes we think we are no longer able to help anyone else, and that we only have enough energy to help ourselves.

We have to consider the balance of health, and the possibility of serving others, but God takes care of the balance for us in our older ages.

You know from reading this book, the great physical suffering I have had. God knows us better than anyone else does. In fact, he knows all of us better than we know ourselves. He knows what we are capable of. Even with my very physically-debilitating health issues through the years, he still asked me to work for him.

I now know why he called me. It is because of my specific experiences with suffering and pain, motherhood, and business experience. He called me to help others sort out life's daily problems and pain, while walking with Our Lord.

God has more confidence in us than we will ever have in ourselves. I know this is true, because he has already told me to do many things I thought were not possible by me, that I thought I was incapable of.

If I had *not* trusted him, I would *not* have been able to carry through with his will for me.

If you remember, I doubted God once, at the time when no religious order would take me. Then I doubted the calling from Jesus. I do not doubt him anymore.

Following the journey of this book, I think you can see how God sorted out my life, one step at a time.

Stay in prayer, trust him, be patient, persevere, and be courageous. Everything will fall in place, in the way God wants it to. His plan is always best. I finally learned this truth, through my own experiences with him!

One must *choose to change*, to commit to help others. If not us baby boomers, then who? The Christian foundation of this country is in dire need of reinforcements.

Join a Christian ministry team, start a food pantry, volunteer at a halfway house, be a CASA advocate,[119] read books to nursing home seniors, console abandoned babies at the local hospital, adopt or foster children, evangelize the faith in some way, donate clothing to detention centers for inmates who will be released, pen pal with an inmate to lift their spirits and give them hope to reform themselves, work at a pregnancy resource center, join a Kairos Prison Ministry Team,[120] and the list goes on and on. There are many people in need, spiritually, mentally, physically, and emotionally. *They are all around us.*

We possess gifts of time, talent, and treasure, which can help others. Even if it is in some small way, it is something. And when everyone helps, the impact is much greater than trying to serve alone.

Like Father Brian said after the calling, and before I retired, "What are you waiting for?" Oh, the power of his words!

In the book of Revelation, we read, "And he who sat upon the throne said, 'Behold, I make all things new.' Also, 'Write this, for these words are trustworthy and true'" (Rev. 21:5).

God renews us *if we let him*. Again, those arrogant words, *if we let him.*

During the COVID-19 shelter-in-place, trying to cobble together the contents of this book, Jesus walked with me through my entire faith journey again. I wrote this book,

---

[119] CASA – Court Appointed Special Advocate Guardians Ad Litem for Children. Learn more at: *www.nationalcasagal.org.*

[120] For more information, visit www.kairosprisonministry.org/index.php.

chapter-by-chapter, with the most significant spiritual events beginning in 2008, when I invited him into my heart with all of my being.

The journey through my past was difficult at times, yet filled with joy other times as well.

Pope Francis said, "The presence of Jesus is everything. There is where the strength of a consecrated vocation is found. It is about getting out of oneself, being passionate about Jesus in love, with a burning heart, and maybe this would become the future for others."[121]

These words of Pope Francis were the intended last words of this book until a couple unexplained mystical encounters happened with the Eucharistic Christ.

Mystical Encounter with the Eucharist

During a daily Mass on Wednesday, January 27, 2021, I witnessed the *actual changing* of the bread (host) into the Precious Body of Jesus Christ. The priest held up the host for all to see, as I have witnessed countless times before. He said, "Behold the Lamb of God, behold him who takes away the sins of the world. Blessed are those called to the supper of the Lamb." At that moment, I noticed a light pink color in the two halves of the host he was holding up over the altar. He had broken them in half, then held them up together. At first, I thought I was seeing a color of the host that was not really there, because normally it is a cream or beige color. After this, we all responded as we normally do, "Lord, I am

---

[121] Pope Francis and Fernando Prado, *The Strength of a Vocation Consecrated Life Today* (United States Conference of Catholic Bishops, 2018).

not worthy that you should enter under my roof, but only say the word and my soul shall be healed."

The priest then dipped the consecrated host into the chalice of the Precious Blood of Jesus and when he took it out of the chalice, the host was a darker pink color. As his hand (with the consecrated host) moved from the chalice towards his mouth to consume it, the Eucharist was mostly red with pink tinges around the edges. I was so taken aback and stunned by what I saw that I drew up my hands together to my chest, whispering "Oh, my God," in a very reverent way, and became breathless for a moment. I was breathless because I could not believe what I was seeing.

As a practicing, devout Catholic, I believe Jesus is present in the Eucharist, and accepted this truth many years ago. I never expected a sign from God to somehow see Our Lord, physically, on the altar, although I read before about this happening.

Much earlier in my faith journey though, I yearned to see some physical sign of Jesus present in the Eucharist. Years ago, I read about unexplained mystical events that took place around the world. There are many accounts of documented Eucharistic miracles.[122] During formation to become a sister, one of our candidates also spoke of seeing the face of Jesus in the monstrance[123] during Eucharistic Adoration. A fellow parishioner shared with me that his sister saw the face of Our Blessed Mother Mary in the same way. It does happen.

God already knows what is in our hearts, and what we yearn for. We must be patient, sometimes waiting for years! If what we

---

[122] Two additional resources on this topic are: *Eucharistic Miracles,* Joan Carroll Cruz (Charlotte, North Carolina: TAN Books, 1987), and *201 Inspirational Stories of the Eucharist,* Sister Patricia Proctor (Spokane, Washington: Poor Clare Sisters, 2004).

[123] Vessel in which the Eucharistic host is carried in processions, or for Eucharistic Adoration.

yearn for is consistent with his will for us, he will give it to us, and in his timing, not ours. But it must be consistent with his will, and if so, it will happen.

I shared this experience with the priest who celebrated the Mass. He said, "Keep this close to your heart." I will not forget this encounter with Jesus. I received an unexpected gift from God, for which I am eternally grateful. I also see this as another confirmation from him, that I should continue to be his hands and feet, doing his will, not mine.

A second unexplained mystical event happened while I was visiting my fellow Sisters in Tijuana, Mexico.

Rose-Scented Eucharist

Tijuana Catholic Church near prison – 2022

On the Feast Day of the Archangels – Michael, Gabriel, and Raphael, September 29, 2022, I received a special gift of God's grace upon my tongue. I was visiting my religious Sisters in Tijuana Mexico for two weeks, to help them, to visit prisoners in the Tijuana prison, to attend a fund raiser, and to spend time with the sisters for the first time in almost three years.

We were attending Mass at what is thought to be one of the oldest churches in Tijuana, that happens to be located close to the prison. When I went to receive communion, I was ready to receive the Eucharist on my tongue, so the palms of my hands were together. The priest opened my hands and placed *two* consecrated hosts in my hand, telling me to eat them. I did, while curious about why he gave me two, instead of one. *At the moment they touched my tongue, I smelled a strong perfume of roses in my mouth.* I had never experienced this before, and had not heard of this happening to anyone.

When we returned to our formation house that morning, I asked the sisters if they received two hosts, and if they smelled roses. Some of the sisters said they received two hosts. *None of the other sisters received what seemed to be a rose-scented host. So, it could not be that the hosts had been perfumed in some way; otherwise, all of us would have smelled roses in the Eucharist we received.*

After I returned home from the trip, I spoke with my spiritual director about this Eucharistic event, and he said that this exact phenomenon happened to him as well, shortly after he was ordained a Catholic priest. The next day, I was in a discussion with a seminarian, as well as another sister who was not at Mass with us that day, and learned that both of them previously had related experiences with the scent of roses.

In discerning what the rose-scented Eucharist was about, my thought was that the Blessed Mother Mary may have also wanted to make her presence known to me in a personal way. We often associate her with roses, or the scent of roses. Did she want to get my attention about something? I am still discerning this. This is the third time she has connected with me in a personal way.

The first time was during a difficult time in formation, when the Blessed Mother spoke to me in the perpetual adoration chapel in the Catholic Church in Buda, Texas, saying "You will have to endure a while longer." More recently, she showed me the Miracle of the Sun at Medjugorje,[124] and

---

[124] To learn more, go to www.medjugorje.org.

shortly after that trip, parts of my Rosary turned gold (it was all silver links prior to this trip).[125]

Then this unexpected rose-scented Eucharist phenomenon happened. My spiritual director believed it was God himself telling me that he loves me. This unexplained mystical phenomenon is something I will never forget. *The scent of roses lasted for a while in my mouth even after I swallowed the Eucharist.*

We must always share our testimony with others.

If I continue to experience unexplained mystical phenomena related to this spiritual autobiography, and I write about these events, when will this book ever get published? So now I must end the writing of this last chapter, and the book.

In closing, this book was prayerfully constructed with the guidance of the Holy Spirit, with multiple themes, to help

---

[125] My oldest son, Chris, gave me this Rosary with jade beads before I was a sister. I lost it five times, and once it broke in the washing machine. Each time I asked St. Anthony to find it for me. He always comes through for us when we are looking for lost things.

others with (1) vocation discernment, (2) conversion of the heart, mind, and soul, (3) a call for volunteerism to help those who suffer, (4) the transition into a consecrated[126] world, and (5) a better understanding of the journey of someone who is called to serve.

And even if none of these categories describe where you are on your faith journey, hopefully this book has been helpful to you in some way.

The discoveries I shared of this spiritual journey are my testimonies, and I included the joy, peace, and fulfillment of accepting God's will for me, that I found along the way. Many of the decisions I made seemed illogical and unreasonable, in the way I used to see things in my former life. I found a plethora of various freedoms in God's illogical ways that I never anticipated, and there are too many to list here.

The list of freedoms will be different for everyone. What are your undiscovered freedoms?

It takes time, patience, perseverance, and courage, to discover these freedoms. Go into the silence, be still, and ask God to reveal his will for you. Then be patient and continue to pray unceasingly. He will tell you, or show you, one step at a time. Do not lose hope.

The steps God gives you may not make sense. They may seem to be illogical and unreasonable ways. Surprisingly, later he will reveal to you that in fact, his ways are logical and reasonable, seen through the lens of a faith-filled Christian. The irony is learning that we are the ones who are illogical and unreasonable, not God!

Writing this book had its own journey of discoveries along the way. The most surprising parts were (1) discovering one morning when I began to write chapter 13, that Jesus wanted me to write about the need for more spiritual leaders

---

[126] A calling may also be for men to become ordained priests or deacons.

to help end the killing of unborn babies; and (2) inviting baby boomers to get more involved in helping our country, with its' many needs for volunteerism.

When I finished writing the first draft, I did not understand how unborn babies (chapter 13) and an invitation to baby boomers (chapter 14) had anything to do with a spiritual autobiography, increasing vocations, and conversions of the heart, mind, and soul (chapters 1-12).

God connected the dots for me, as he always does. We need more religious vocations who are leaders and true to their faith. This book helps readers to discern if they have a religious vocation, and what to do about it. This includes learning the work that is involved in experiencing a conversion of the heart, mind, and soul, as they journey towards ordination or religious consecration.

Once there are more religious leaders (new vocations) who are truly loyal and faithful to the Gospels of God's Word, we might stand a better chance of bringing our country back to God, and we might begin to reverse the course of this country's spiritual decline. Until we have leaders who are convicted in the true Christian faith, based upon the values and virtues of Jesus Christ, with a sense of moral focus in all things, we will continue to die, spiritually, as a society.

Did you notice how this book began with a story of the Precious *Blood* of Jesus (in the preface)? Did you notice that the essence of these last stories of this chapter is about the Precious *Body* of Jesus? Do you think this is a coincidence? Does this remind you of the alpha and the omega?

In Revelation 22:13, Jesus said, "I am the Alpha and the Omega, the first and the last, the beginning and the end." And in Revelation 22:12, Jesus said, "Behold, I am coming soon, bringing my recompense, to repay every one for what he has done."

In the *Last Drop* story in the preface of this book, Jesus said to me, *"If there are no priests left anywhere in the world, then I will have to come back."*

Do you wonder if you have a religious calling? Or are you called to serve others in another way? If you consider a religious vocation, whether you are young, or in your later years of life, it will be natural for obstacles to get in your way. Pray, persevere, discern, and keep going.

Even if you do not have a calling to serve as ordained or consecrated, consider giving of yourself to help humanity in some significant way.

Our world needs you in *any* way you can give of yourself. Follow your own journey of discoveries that God has already planned for you, and find freedom in God's illogical ways.

Final question for the reader to contemplate: Will I let God change me, to grow spiritually, to become a new version of myself, who he is still waiting for, to help bring others to his son, Jesus, and away from evil?

The End

or…

The Beginning

ACKNOWLEDGEMENTS

Who helped me write this book? Jesus Christ. He pulled out of me what he specifically wanted written in this book. He told me what to write until it was complete. When he stopped telling me what to do, the writing of the *first draft* of this book, ended. I felt a sense of completion and fulfillment. And I realized we created something good together, even though it was only a rough draft.

I am not a theologian, ordained minister, or a spiritual director, yet the Holy Spirit provided me with divine promptings to stir my soul on this journey of discoveries, and in ways I have never experienced.

It takes a village to write and publish a book. God sent me many effective and experienced messengers, and talented professional people throughout this process.

Six months before I began writing this book, I was waiting at a detention center with a fellow prison ministry team member, Judy Hausmann, to begin our ministry for the night. I shared with her that Jesus told me to write a book, but I had no idea of what I was doing. She asked me if I wanted help. I said yes! Shortly thereafter, I received a call from her good friend, Lyn Stowers, *a publishing industry retiree!* What are the odds of *that* happening?

There are no coincidences in the lives of faithful believers. God sent these special messengers to me during the times I needed them.

Lyn and I talked for an hour, while I shared details of my faith journey, and in the middle of the conversation, she said, *"Sister, you have to write this book!"*

I had no confidence in what I was doing, because I never wrote a book before; however, I trusted that in God's providence, he would give me his grace to fulfill his will for me. What was I concerned about?

While Lyn read the first draft, I held my breath (not literally of course), waiting for her assessment. I thought my first draft was horrible. She said it was good. Lyn was supportive of me from the beginning, guiding me through this daunting and unfamiliar process. Grateful seems to be an inadequate expression for her sincere and unending support.

Other pivotal players have been the Delegate of the Archbishop of Tijuana, Father John Howard, CJM; Steve Marshall, Eudist Theologian and Mission Advancement Director, both of The Eudists – Congregation of Jesus and Mary (CJM); and Sister Viola Ramirez, General Leader of the Eudist Servants of the Eleventh Hour (ESEH). Father John Howard expressed that *this work is "worthy of publishing" and to "give talks and interviews to speak of God's work and grace for you."* Sister Viola Ramirez recognized the amount of work that went into the writing of the book. I am very grateful for all of their support.

Steve Marshall is not only the Eudist Theologian who conducts spiritual retreats for the sisters at our annual gatherings in Tijuana, Mexico, but he is also in charge of publishing for Eudist Press International, and is the Mission Advancement Director for the Eudists – Congregation of Jesus and Mary. He was instrumental in educating me on their publishing process. Steve is an active listener, kind, patient, flexible and brilliant. He genuinely exudes the light of Christ in all things, generating all his work for the glory of God. I am thankful he is the leader of the village it has taken to publish this book. After he read a later revision of the manuscript, he expressed genuine joy over what Jesus and I wrote in this book. As he said in one of his emails to me, *"I just can't wait to get it out there."* I am very grateful for the professional work of Steve and his publishing team.

Steve's professional editor, Emily Deady, provided the thorough scrub this work needed. It is difficult to find the words of appreciation for her dedicated efforts. Her efforts gave me the peace of mind that a first-time author needs to proceed with publishing!

Tom Peterson, host of the Eternal Word Television Network (EWTN) TV show, *Catholics Come Home*, generously provided his explicit insight on marketing literary works, for which I am extremely grateful. I have experience in many areas of business, but marketing is not one of them.

My youngest sister, Mary McDonald, had the heavenly patience to capture and illustrate the vision of the book cover that the Holy Spirit gave me. Her dedication, listening ear, and artistic eye for detail, produced an accurate depiction of the vision. Her talent is unlimited!

And it has been a joy-filled journey to listen to how the "first readers" felt after they read earlier drafts of the book. I am appreciative of their feedback and support. With each reading of the draft by these readers, and listening to their comments, I began to see what Jesus wanted to accomplish through me; that is, a book that would provide answers, warm hearts, give hope, and see joy through the spiritual autobiographical journey of a Catholic sister.

APPENDIX A – RECOMMENDED READING LIST

—✶—

Church Resources

> The Holy Bible, Revised Standard Version, Second Catholic Edition (Nashville, Tennessee: Thomas Nelson, 1966)
> Pope Francis, *Gaudete Et Exsultate: On the Call to Holiness in Today's World* (2018)
> Pope Saint John Paul II, *Evangelium Vitae: The Gospel of Life* (1995)
> YOUCAT: Youth Catechism of the Catholic Church (2011)

Devotional and/or Biography

> Sarah Young, *Jesus Calling* (Thomas Nelson, 2004)
> *Little Books* series from the Diocese of Saginaw
> Adorers of the Precious Blood, *Precious Blood of Jesus Daily Devotional* (Precious Blood International, 2007)
> Lyle W. Dorsett, *The Life of D.L. Moody: Passion for Souls* (Moody Publishers, 2003)
> Pope Francis & Fernando Prado, CMF, *The Strength of a Vocation: Consecrated Life Today* (USCCB, 2018)

On Mother Antonia and Saint John Eudes

- ➢ Mary Jordan & Kevin Sullivan, The Prison Angel: Mother Antonia's Journey from Beverly Hills to a Life of Service in a Mexican Jail (Penguin, 2006)
- ➢ *La Mama: An American Nun's Life In A Mexican Prison* (Jody Hammond, 2010)
- ➢ Saint John Eudes, *Eudist Prayerbook Series* (Eudist Press International, 2015-2021)
- ➢ Bishop Clement Guillon, *In All Things, the Will of God: Saint John Eudes Through His Letters* (Eudist Press International, 2019)

On Spiritual Warfare

- ➢ Father Gabriele Amorth, *My Battle Against Satan* (Sophia Institute Press, 2018)
- ➢ Adam C. Blai, *Possession, Exorcisms, and Hauntings* (Emmaus Road, 2017)
- ➢ Doctor Paul Thigpen, *Manual for Spiritual Warfare* (Tan Books, 2014)

APPENDIX B – INDEX OF PRAYERS/MEDITATIONS USED

APPENDIX C – TRANSITION FROM INCARCERATED TO HOME

⚊⁄₁⧹⚊

Problem Solving with Spirituality - Transition from Incarcerated to Home

(Authored by Charles and Linda Johnston)

Scripture References:

I Peter 5:8   Be sober-minded; be watchful. Your adversary the devil prowls around like a roaring lion, seeking someone to devour.

I Timothy 4:1 Now the spirit expressly says that in later times some will depart from the faith by devoting themselves to deceitful spirits and teachings of demons.

Psalm 23   The Lord is my shepherd; I shall not want. He maketh me to lie down in green pastures: he leadeth me beside the still waters. He restoreth my soul: he leadeth me in the paths of righteousness for his name's sake. Yea, though I walk through the valley of the shadow of death, I will fear no evil: for thou art with me; thy rod and thy staff they comfort me. Thou preparest a table before me in the presence of mine enemies: thou anointest my head with oil; my cup runneth over. Surely goodness and mercy shall follow me all the days of my life: and I will dwell in the house of the Lord forever.

<u>Discussion: Preparing to Go Home</u>: You must remember and never forget that our Heavenly Father loves you and protects you all the time. In your preparation, meditation and prayer are vitally important. You now have the tools necessary to fulfill a life full of joy, faith, charity, and love. What have you done to prepare yourself for a new beginning?

<u>Discussion: What to Expect Once Home</u>: You have been away from home for some time and many people are disappointed in you, including yourself. You must remember that Christ has forgiven you through His crucifixion. Therefore, through prayer and remembrance of Christ, you can hold your head up high. What are the obstacles that you face once home?

<u>Discussion: Commitment to Change</u>: What lead you to be incarcerated must cease. The old ways did not work and will not work in the future. You are not a "loser." You have a great opportunity to be a role model in your community or family to show that one can overcome the obstacles of the evil one through God's love and mercy. Are you really committed to change?

<u>Discussion: Establishing Trust and Rebuilding Bridges</u>: We tend to believe that our presence alone is enough to wipe out people's fears and disappointments in us. That is not true. You must work every day to slowly build the trust that people once had in you. This rebuilding of bridges is a slow process. You cannot expect to get back all those relationships and all those you have hurt. However, through time, patience, good behavior, and love you are setting the groundwork for healing. How can I build trust and rebuild bridges?

<u>Discussion: Resources Available to Keep Me Out of Trouble</u>: Sometimes we are too stubborn to ask for help but believe it or not, there are those that in doing God's work, love to help people like you and programs specifically directed

at any problems you may have, i.e., Alcoholics Anonymous, Narcotics Anonymous, NAMI (National Association of Mental Illness), social services, churches, Catholic Charities, food banks, Department of Labor, etc. Do you know what resources are available to you?

Discussion: Settling Into a New Life: Many of you will be on probation for many years and look at this as a negative. Random drug tests, payments must be made, and some probation officers can generate fear and anger in you. This is where you can turn a "negative into a positive." Your probation officer has a wealth of knowledge—what services are available, how to find a job, and listening to your problems (like having your own personal counselor). If you stay clean and out of trouble, you will find probation manageable. How will I deal with probation?

Discussion: Crisis Management: There are going to be times, leave it to the evil one, where you will be tempted to go back to your "old ways." You may be angry, restless, or bored. HALT—are you hungry, angry, lonely, or tired? This is where it is so important to take time out and ask for God's help. Not everything is going to turn out the way you want it to. You must use your resources, especially from those people who are living a righteous life. Become friends with people at church and become close to someone you trust who leads a good life. Call them and ask for help. Lose your pride and do all that is necessary to avoid coming back here. With God's love and an open heart, you will be able to handle any crisis that arises. Can you foresee a crisis?

Discussion: A Look Forward: Now that you have established yourself back in your community, it is important to remember the blessings that God has given you. There is an old saying, "You can't keep it unless you give it away." There are many people who need your help. You have unique experiences—you must express them in volunteerism. Helping others is one of the greatest gifts you can give yourself and bestow upon your fellow man. Once I am settled in, how can I help in my community?

ABOUT THE AUTHOR

Photo by my granddaughter, Olivia Power

At the age of 56, she retired as a federal government manager, leaving behind a six-figure salary and great benefits, to make drastic changes in her life. Was this logical or reasonable? She had experience in accounting, finance, policy, procedures, real estate, supervision, and management. What was it that enticed a Veteran, mother, grandmother, and successful business woman, who still had a bright future ahead of her, to chase after something greater than the life she achieved?

For questions and comments about this book, contact Sister Mary Francis Power at srmaryfrancispower@gmail.com.

Women who would like to inquire about becoming a sister with the Eudist Servants of the Eleventh Hour, please go to www.eudistservants.org.

Men who would like to inquire about becoming a priest with the Congregation of Jesus and Mary (Eudist Fathers), please go to www.eudistsusa.org.

Donations may be made at these websites.

Made in the USA
Las Vegas, NV
27 December 2023

83622725R00167